MANUEL

MANUEL

A Totonac Indian's changed life is a tribute to the persistence and courage of the Wycliffe Bible Translators.

Hugh Steven

FLEMING H. REVELL COMPANY
OLD TAPPAN, NEW JERSEY

Fourth Printing

Published by Fleming H. Revell Company

Library of Congress Catalog Card Number: 73-123060
Printed in the United States of America

TO

Herman and Bessie Aschmann
and to the great company of
Wycliffe translators around the world
who are making other Manuels possible.

Contents

Preface

To the casual observer, the hundred and fifty thousand Totonac Indians of southeastern Mexico appear happy and ideally suited to their environment. Totonac men, neatly dressed in white, unbleached muslin, tip their palm hats to waving motorists traveling along the highways to Pozarica, Tuxpan and Papantla. Barefoot, brown-skinned Totonac women, in flowing white skirts and colorfully embroidered blouses, walk their mountain trails with the grace and poise of ballerinas.

Totonacs, whose ancestors are said by some experts to have been first to greet Cortez, seem to live unburdened by the ponderous problems associated with modern society. Actually, the reverse is true. Many Totonacs are compulsive drinkers, and hundreds of men and women become hopeless alcoholics by their mid-twenties. After a village fiesta, it is not uncommon to observe many of the women sleeping off a drunken stupor in the tall grass beside a mountain trail, oblivious to the plaintive cries of the children strapped to their backs.

Totonac men observe the outside world to be different and they are frustrated by that difference. Daily reminders in the form of jet planes, carrying tourists and trade to Veracruz, Yucatán, and the Caribbean, crisscross the air above their mountain villages. Spanish-speaking merchants, unable to learn the long-worded Totonac sentences, make derogatory remarks about Totonacs speaking jibberish and take advantage of the lack of communication.

Few people understand that Totonac is not jibberish but a full, beautiful language with all the components for effective, meaningful communication. According to Jimenez Moreno the classic period of Totonac culture played a vital role in middle American civilization.

The Totonac has retained his own distinct language and culture, and because of this he is unable to interpret accurately the power and fury of the twentieth century. He misunderstands the broad scope of his rights and privileges as a full-fledged Mexican citizen, and there are few people who understand him well enough to become his champion. Language barriers and cultural differences frustrate many governmental agencies and philanthropic societies. The Totonac is therefore exposed to the unprincipled and ruthless who steal, overcharge and exploit.

Totonacs who journey to the outside world seldom return. Life in the big city offers greater rewards. Those few who do return do so as visitors and find themselves strangers to their own culture, unable to identify or deal realistically with village life and problems.

Out of this matrix of land-locked culture has come the hybrid, Manuel Arenas, who in his thirty-eight years has become a legend among the Totonacs and in more than twenty-five countries of the world. He is a man I am proud to call a personal friend.

HUGH STEVEN

Appreciation

I wish to acknowledge, with special thanks, Miss Ethel Wallis, for her ability to spot stories and her belief in me.

To Manuel, who, while suffering much physical discomfort, spent long and patient hours answering questions and giving information. And for being the remarkable person he is!

To each of my colleagues and friends who prayed much for the completion of this book.

To Albert Williams, Ruth Bishop, Herman and Bessie Aschmann for detailed anecdotal material.

To James C. Hefley for professional encouragement and editorial help.

To Mrs. Sylvia Carstens for her typing assistance.

To my secretary, Lyn Fischer, for her enthusiasm about the story and the typing of draft copies.

And finally, special mention to my wife, Norma, for her endless hours of encouragement, for completely giving of herself to editing and typing of the final manuscript. For her love and patience and her faith that I would complete the book. Also to my children, Wendy, David, Lee and Karen, who endured much, who prayed much and are glad it's over!

I would also like to give special thanks to Manuel's host of friends who, for reasons of brevity, could not be mentioned in the book, but who have done much to help Manuel with his education and the establishment of his Bible school.

MANUEL

I

Sweet Bread and Liquor

She noticed first the woven basket full of sweet bread and the jug of corn liquor. They sat in the corner like disciplined school children. The sight curdled the girl's stomach.

Totonac girls expect marriage early, between the ages of twelve and fifteen. They know and accept their role as creatures without choice. When the time for marriage arrives, they know their parents will choose their husbands. The seal of marriage approval is the giving and receiving of liquor and sweet bread.

Twelve-year-old Luz cupped the heels of her hands to her eyes and rubbed out the sleep. She rolled up her straw sleeping mat and put it in a corner of her shelf-like attic. Carefully she placed one small bare foot in the top notch of the pole ladder and descended backwards to the floor of the mud hut.

"Who, little Mother? Who came in the night and brought the sweet bread?" she asked fearfully.

The mother squatted beside the small cooking fire burning in the center of the dirt floor. Expertly she formed pancake-like *tortillas* and placed them on a clay griddle resting on three smoke-blackened stones. Smoke from the fire billowed slowly toward the thick straw roof and hung there under the eaves like a mist.

"Ah," said the mother, "so it is my lazy daughter who asks. Always do you sleep past the rooster's call. But, never mind, soon you will rise before he calls."

"What do you mean, little Mother?" asked Luz. "The sweet bread and liquor—does it mean I am promised to be married?"

Luz's mother wiped her nose with the back of her hand. "Yes, my little Luz. Your uncle came in the night and told us that Mariano wishes you for his wife."

Luz winced when she heard the name Mariano. Orphaned at six months and cared for by Luz's kindly but doting uncle, Mariano grew to his fifteen years a spoiled, selfish, undisciplined child.

"But, little Mother," pleaded Luz, "I have only twelve years. I care not for Mariano. I have no feeling inside for him. All my feeling is for Alejandro. He is the one I wish to marry."

Luz knew the strict Totonac tribal law forbade girls and boys of marriageable age to speak more than just a greeting to each other. But somehow Luz had forgotten all tribal and family laws when Alejandro had waited at the water hole and asked her for a drink from her jug. Especially had she forgotten when he brought her wild orchids from the forest and helped her gather firewood. Luz had thought what a good husband he would make!

"For you to have no feeling inside," said her mother angrily, "is not important. Mariano is liked by your father and by me. We do not like Alejandro. You will marry after the Fiesta of All Saints."

Luz's pleas to her mother to select Alejandro for her husband were like droplets of water on hot stones. They evaporated in the steam of strong reproaches accompanied by a stiff slap across her delicate mouth.

"It's a sin to speak to a boy before marriage. Say not a word to your father or you will feel the weight of his tumpline across your back. Go now to the river and wash the corn. Take your small brother also so I can know if you talk with Alejandro."

Luz lifted one of the hand-hewn plank boards that served as a door, pushed it aside, and slipped through the opening into the cold predawn darkness. Though her body was still that of a child, there was an ease and beauty in her carriage that suggested the presence of an unusual character. Gracefully she lifted a basket of yellow corn upon her small head and started for the river. If the trail she selected was the longest, it was also the most scenic. And it was the least traveled. Twelve-year-old Totonac girls are not supposed to cry, and it would not be right for anyone to see the silver tear that rested on the crest of her high cheekbone.

Luz loved this trail to the river. A few steps into the jungle forest and the chorus of unorganized sounds of barking dogs, crying babies and the pittypat of women making tortillas was blotted out. Here sweetly singing nightingales, canaries, robins and cedar waxwings mingled their voices with the chirps of colorfully plumed parrots, macaws and an entourage of tropical birds.

For a moment Luz forgot her heartbreak and lingered, breathing in the odor of pungent vanilla orchids. As she walked the trail it was as if some huge hand had placed each giant cedar along the path in perfect order and then as an afterthought, had decked the branches with long vertical vines, each one aflame with giant orange, blue and red trumpet flowers. In her reverie, she hardly noticed the tug on her long skirt.

"Our mother will become angry," said her little brother. "She will wonder if you talk to Alejandro. We must hurry. The Feast of All Saints is but seven days from now and there is much to be done."

The village president lifted the thick brown book off a dusty shelf and laid it on a rough wooden table stained with ink blotches, candle wax and the rings left by soda pop bottles.

"It is good you obey the law of the Republic and come for the civil marriage first," said the president, rubbing his stubbled chin. With a great show of authority he had Luz's parents stand in front of his desk.

An important place, this dirt-floored courthouse! In a village of over two thousand people, it was the only building that contained paper, ink and a typewriter. No matter that the typewriter was without a ribbon and old enough to be a museum piece. It belonged to the village, and everyone was proud to say that his town hall had a typewriter.

Luz stood to one side of the desk with Mariano beside her. Her head was bowed; her jet eyes stared down in glassy disbelief at what was happening to her. She looked pathetic and, by other standards, over-dressed. A flowing white dress reached to her ankles. The white embroidered blouse was tucked into a maroon sash that was much too wide for her small waist. Around her long, delicate neck she wore six strands of mixed yellow, red, blue, and orange glass beads. Her black hair was parted in the middle of her tiny head and was drawn tightly back into two thick pigtails that hung to below the small of her back. There they were tied together by the two-colored yellow-and-orange ribbon woven through each pigtail. From her wafer-thin ears hung tear-shaped, hand-worked silver earrings. Over all, and to her knees was a white lace shawl.

Mariano's blouse, shirt, and pantaloons were completely white, as was the kerchief around his thick, bronzed neck. His black hair, starting just above his eyebrows, was plastered with grease and fighting to regain its normal porcupine appearance.

After noisily clearing his throat, the president began by telling Mariano it would now be his responsibility to make a cornfield of his own and provide money and shelter for his new wife. He ended a long list of duties by asking the groom if he loved Luz, to which Mariano nodded shyly. Turning to Luz, the president read a list of wifely duties that included such important items as gathering firewood, getting up early to prepare the corn bread, and not burning the *tortillas.* When the president came to the routine question, "Do you love Mariano?" Luz lifted her head and looked at the president.

There was a long moment of silence. Then before Mariano and the parents knew what had happened, Luz screamed a defiant "No!" and raced out of the courthouse and up the hill to her hut to wait for the inevitable.

Sooner than she expected, her father bolted through the door and wrenched his woven tumpline off the wall. Without a word, he plunged it into the jug and waited until the fibers became swollen and heavy.

Luz crouched in a corner, saying not a word but pleading desperately with her eyes for her father not to strike her. With the first blow she knew her father's anger was uncontrollable. Blow after blow fell on her slender body, and they ceased only when her father became exhausted. It then became her mother's turn to resume the unmerciful beating. Only when the mother wearied did the punishment end. As he walked out of the house the father called back, "Next time the president asks if you love Mariano you will say yes!"

Three days later when she was barely able to stand upright Luz nodded to the stern question of the president. At that point the names of Mariano and Luz Vasquez Arenas were recorded in large script in the village record book. There was one final ceremony before the marriage would be legal. It would have to be solemnized by the priest.

"Do you love Mariano?" asked the priest in his turn.

She lifted her head to answer. The simple movement caused her pain, but she also knew that life with Mariano would mean continual pain. In one final effort to convince her parents she did not want this union Luz said, "No, I have no feeling inside for Mariano. I do not love him!" And for the second time in three days, Luz ran from the presence of undisputed authority.

"It was my uncle who saved me," as Luz would tell the story in later life. "My father was angry like a bull and again he beat me until I no longer felt the blows."

"If you must beat something, beat me," said the small, but husky man standing quietly in the doorway. Her uncle was the village leader. Presidents were elected, but it was this quiet, solid little barefoot man who made the final decisions.

"Is it not unwise to force Luz to marry at this time?" he said quietly. "At fifteen she will want to be a wife, and Mariano at eighteen will be a better husband. To save your honor and not be disgraced by the return of the gifts let them marry, but let Luz live in her own house with you until she has fifteen years."

It was an unusual request, but it made sense to her parents and they agreed. On her fifteenth birthday Luz was still unhappy but she was unable to fight the pressure of tribal tradition and so submitted.

One daughter and two sons were born to Luz in rapid succession. Each birth was assisted by the unwashed hands of Totonac midwives. When the time came for the fourth delivery, it was dark and cold and raining. Inside the hut a small fire in the middle of the dirt floor flickered each time the damp wind squeezed through the upright poles that formed the walls of the hut. Mariano slept on a thin straw mat laid on a raised, wooden platform. Three children also slept on straw mats, but near the fire. Close to the doorway three older women squatted on their cracked, leather-tough heels. They whispered of their achievements as women who had helped with most of the village births.

Luz was in the corner opposite her husband. She also was squatted on her heels, her back against the wall. While the children huddled close for warmth in the thirty-degree temperature, large beads of perspiration glistened on Luz's bronze forehead. Her small hands clutched a rope that hung from pole beams supporting the straw roof. With each pain, Luz gave the customary thrust with her pelvis. Then out of a deep blackness blinding her eyes and pain that screamed from every tissue of her small body, she bore a son.

Quickly the old women sprang into action. One woman cut two long tassels from her shawl and deftly tied the throbbing cord. Another woman held an old machete over the fire until the blade was black and then expertly severed the life line, separating mother and child. At the first wail Mariano lifted himself on one arm and wearily asked what it was.

"A son to work your cornfields," said one of the midwives.

"Ah, a son. The gods are good. His name will be Leopoldo." With that, he drew the thin blanket over his shoulders and returned to sleep.

Luz, exhausted but happy, took the child and nuzzled his wrinkled ear and whispered, "You will be Leopoldo to your father, but I will call you Manuel."

2

House of Dreams

Six-year-old Manuel loosened his sweaty grip on his mother's hand and carefully bent himself in half. In quiet disbelief he gently patted the tile of the patio floor.

Luz waited nervously until her new Mexican employer led her through a large dining room, which she noted, was a place where people sat to eat; past a kitchen, which she noticed as a place where people stood to cook; and then into a room off the back patio. There she saw a large pile of dirty clothes. Without a word, Luz gathered them up and began her awkward retreat through rooms that were each larger than two Indian huts.

In her excitement about her thirty-two cent per week laundry job, Luz had forgotten Manuel. Now, fearful of offending her Mexican mistress, Luz called softly, but anxiously, for Manuel to join her. She knew from past experience that her son's explosive curiosity would compel him to feel, smell and touch each item his small hands could find. She was surprised to find him almost where she had left him. In his hands he held a store-bought top and three glass marbles—priceless treasures for a Totonac boy whose toy marbles were the small gray seeds Totonac women gathered along the riverbank and made into necklaces.

"If you want people to respect your things," Luz told him, "you must learn to respect theirs." Her tone of voice was such that Manuel even at this age knew obedience was the better part of valor. He put the marbles and top down on the patio floor and followed his mother to the river.

Luz found a place where the river had torn out a section of the riverbank, leaving a spoon-shaped pool. Without pausing until her work was done, she rubbed each garment with a broad, green leaf that secreted a thick soapy substance, rinsed and wrung it in river water, and laid it out to dry on the chalk-colored river rocks. From a distance, the drying clothes appeared as a huge patchwork quilt.

Meanwhile, Manuel cavorted about like a frog, diving and swimming in the deep pools. Now and then he left the water to search for the gray seed marbles. Each time he found one he could not help feeling disappointed they were not glass. The large Mexican house, with its orange-colored tile roof and blue cement walls, within which he had found a store-bought top and glass marbles, had become his house of dreams.

Bored now with his water games, Manuel scrambled up the riverbank, hurriedly pulled on his white pantaloons, and stuck the faded palm sombrero on his head. "L–l–little Mother," he said, shivering and sucking in short breaths of air, "I–I–I would like a top that comes from a store."

"Gather wood for fires," said Luz quickly, "and if you sell it, save your money for a top." Gathering firewood to sell was a new idea for Manuel and he smiled.

After the sun had dried and bleached the garments, Luz

rolled them into a bundle which she swung onto her back. "Come, little son," she said. "I must yet iron these clothes before dark. You can help by fanning the fire with your sombrero to keep the coals hot for the iron."

Luz ironed all afternoon and into the early evening. She rubbed the stubby flatiron over each garment, being careful not to press too hard when the iron was first removed from the heat. After the iron cooled, she returned it to the black charcoal brazier. It then became Manuel's job to fan the coals vigorously with his sombrero. For a time Manuel was happy with the importance of his chore, but by late afternoon the novelty had worn off. By then all he could think of was the large basket of sweet bread sitting unattended on the kitchen counter.

"Maybe," thought Manuel, "the people of this house will give me a piece of sweet bread." His breakfast at six-thirty that morning consisted of three *tortillas* washed down with a cup of lukewarm coffee sweetened with *panela.* His lunch was three more *tortillas,* this time washed down with cold river water.

It soon became obvious to Manuel that the Mexican family had no intention of sharing its sweet bread or any of its food with him or his mother. From his perch atop a rain barrel Manuel could see into the dining area. The room, illuminated by a single overhead lamp, seemed brighter than he imagined a room could be. And never had he seen such food! A maid set two large white serving bowls of steaming black beans on the table between a tall stack of *tortillas* wrapped in a white cloth and a large platter of fried Mexican rice cooked in tomato sauce. The maid then served each member of the family of six a large portion of fried beefsteak topped with onions. Manuel remembered his last taste of meat, a thin piece of chicken rolled in a corn-meal *tamale* at the Fiesta of All Saints three months before. He swallowed. The sting of garlic, onion, and tomatoes mixed with the strong smell of herbs churned the dull hunger-ache in his stomach until he felt sick.

"Come, little son," said Luz. "We must return to our own house and prepare food for the return of your father. Let us hope he is not too filled with corn liquor."

Back in the family hut, Manuel ate his meal seated on a small three-legged stool near the fire. He sipped warm coffee from a battered enamel cup. Now and then he dipped a piece of *tortilla* into an enamel dish and spooned up a mouthful of black beans. As he chewed he stared into space. "I wonder," he thought, "why our house doesn't have a tile roof."

In the year that followed Manuel's first visit to his house of dreams, he was made aware on numerous occasions of the existence of a great wall between himself and the children of the house. One such episode made a lasting impression. One day early in his association an overpowering urge moved him to ask one of the boys for a piece of candy. The Mexican boy laughed, but then, as though on second thought, he offered the candy to Manuel. Just as Manuel reached for it, however, the boy snatched the candy back. "Ha," he said with a sneer. "Only people with crazy heads give candy to animals." The boy laughed again and popped the candy into his mouth.

Brokenhearted, and running all the way, Manuel fled up the long trail to his favorite hideout, a large flat rock that jutted out into space like the spur on a fighting cock. Near spent, he crawled out to where he could see his village of Zapotitlán a thousand feet below. The Totonac huts looked sad and lonely. The few Mexican houses appeared menacing. "Why," he wondered, "do people act unfriendly when they live in a stone house?"

The aerie was Manuel's refuge in time of anguish and a magic carpet when he wanted to dream. Here he wondered about the world beyond the craggy mountain barriers and about the airplanes that flew over them. Now, he wondered about the difference between Totonacs and Mexicans. "Why?" he questioned aloud. "Why will the Mexican boy not share? If I would be the boy from that family and had too much, I would divide it in half and give to someone else."

Manuel never understood why his mother wouldn't buy him sweet bread with the money she made washing clothes. "We can buy only important things," she would reply. "With this money I must buy our salt, *chili, panela,* and coffee." The question and answer were repeated over and over without resolution. But more devastating than not being able to afford sweet bread, was not being able to buy the top he had saved for.

In almost a year's time Manuel had chopped down and carried back to the village large quantities of firewood for the cooking fires of his neighbors. In Totonac fashion he had placed each coin he received in payment in a jug buried in a secret spot in his backyard. Just before the important Fiesta of the New Year, Manuel told his mother he had enough money to buy the top.

Luz faced her son sadly and said, "Manuel, in our sad house there is never enough for food and clothes. Your father drinks away the money we need for food. You cannot buy the top. It is wrong to spend money on things that cannot be used. And you, my son, need a sombrero before a top."

The one-room school in Zapotitlán was presided over by a kindly old teacher named Maestro Pepino. He had white hair and three gold teeth; he spoke Totonac and was loved by everyone. But in the wake of inevitable change, a new teacher came to the village. This one spoke only Spanish. Some said he could speak Totonac but believed Spanish was the language for educated people.

The new teacher reinforced his lessons by repeatedly cracking his knuckles on the skulls of the students, who sat dumb at his questions in Spanish. After a particularly trying day during which many a head had been bruised, Manuel and his schoolmates held a council of war.

After much talk it was decided that a large pit should be dug along the path behind the school leading to the outhouse. The path was narrow and ran between a cornfield and an irrigation ditch. There would be no way to avoid the pit. Early that evening, Manuel and three of his friends dug a hole three feet square and eight to nine feet deep. To make the prank more rewarding, the boys filled the hole with water from the irrigation ditch. Then a thin lattice of branches was made to cover the hole. For good measure the boys scattered leaves over the branches and left for home. For Manuel, sleep that night was impossible. In the morning Luz wondered why he left the hut before his customary *tortillas* and coffee.

Strategically placed in a large tree near the hole, Manuel and his companions waited for the golden moment of revenge. Then it happened. The new teacher walked slowly down the path absent-mindedly cleaning his glasses. At one point he paused and looked around, then slowly continued his morning constitutional and stepped into the hole!

It was almost impossible for the boys not to laugh, but somehow they strangled the impulse to do so. They wanted to be sure their quarry could not escape before they showed themselves. Manuel saw the teacher grasp and slip as he tried frantically to claw his way up the slimy clay sides of the hole. The boys almost fell out of the tree when the teacher tried to inch his way up by putting his back and legs on the walls. For a moment Manuel thought he might make it, but he failed and crashed back into the dirty brown water. Finally in desperation the teacher began to yell for help.

"Socorro! Socorro!" he yelled. "Someone is trying to kill me!"

At this, Manuel and his friends, unable to contain themselves a moment longer, began to laugh. It was a long moment before they could control themselves. "We will help you," they said at last. "But first you must promise never to hit our heads again."

The embarrassed teacher made a reluctant promise to Manuel and his companions. Only then did the boys bring a ladder for their imprisoned teacher.

Manuel's mother, on her return from the morning market, heard about the teacher's plight. "Did you hear what happened to your teacher?" said Luz to Manuel when she found him munching quietly on his *tortillas.*

"No," said Manuel innocently. "What happened?"

Luz related the story as she had heard it from the local grapevine. Then added, "And they did it to kill him!"

"I don't think people wanted to kill him," said Manuel knowingly.

Quickly Luz put the facts together. "How did you know?" she demanded. "Did you partake in this?"

Manuel feared a spanking, but he also knew he could not fool his mother. "Yes," he said, his face firm and unsmiling, "but first I am going to tell you why."

After Manuel's explanation, Luz thought for a moment, then said sternly, "I will not spank you for telling the truth but it is very wrong what you have done."

The single event of the year that gave to Manuel a faint glimmer of his noble Totonac heritage was the Fiesta of the New Year. The marking of this symbolic passage of time is met with unusual soberness in Totonac homes. Idols that have been neglected during the year are dusted off and set in a place of honor. On New Year's Eve the devout abstain from liquor, smoking, the opposite sex, cursing and bad thoughts, believing that each day of the new year will be a continuance of this one virtuous night.

To reinforce the symbol of purity, Totonac men outfit themselves in completely new wardrobes. If on New Year's Day a Totonac man is seen with a patch in his *calzónes* or wearing his old sombrero, it is immediately known (to his shame) that here is a man who has not prayed to the idols.

It was because of Luz's strong faith in the idols that she gathered her family to pray, not only on New Year's Eve, but every day. On this night six wooden idols, each about eighteen inches in height, occupied the place of honor in

Manuel's house. Sitting cross-legged, the assembled family repeated the prayers after Luz, but in a perfunctory fashion, without feeling or understanding.

"I wonder," thought Manuel, "why the idols never move."

From seven to thirteen, Manuel's life was a carbon of countless Totonac boys before him, except that Manuel possessed a fiery curiosity about life beyond the deep green canyons that hemmed his mountain village. The little schooling he received awakened a thirst for knowledge. Manuel's father, however, scoffed at the pretense of school and forced Manuel to leave. "You will always be an ignorant Totonac," said Mariano. "Who can understand the Spanish words of a Mexican teacher? It is better to learn how to become a man and cultivate corn and coffee."

Mariano himself never understood the meaning of becoming a man. When early in his marriage he was jailed for conspiracy in a murder plot, the humiliating experience had no lasting effect whatsoever on his character. He continued an arrogant little man full of his own self-importance. Manuel never understood why his mother was forced into such a painful union. Alongside the lithe, graceful Luz, Mariano appeared the caricature of a gnome married to a jewelled princess.

Home was where Mariano dragged himself after drinking bouts with his friends. On these occasions, he was a grotesque blob of alcoholic blubber. When sober he brutally gratified his animal instincts without love, respect or tenderness.

Mariano's other pastime was to beat his children for minor offenses. Once he asked Manuel to bring him the bananas Luz had bought in the market. Manuel started to explain (according to previous instruction from Luz) that they were for the evening meal. Before he had finished, Mariano exploded in a white rage and began to lash the boy with the ever-present tumpline. So severe was the beating that Manuel lay on his straw mat for several days.

3

Flower of Death

Freshened by a night of pelting rain, the world sparkled like dew in the morning sun. To Manuel in his aerie the cornfields seemed like stepping stones to the valley far below, each appearing as a tiny patch shaved out of the stubble of the jungle by a giant razor. To plant and harvest their corn the men of Zapotitlán frequently had to anchor themselves with ropes to available trees. This prevented them from literally falling out of their cornfields.

Manuel sighed, inhaled a generous gulp of fresh air and turned on his back to watch the white clouds sailing overhead. He lay and let the sun etch a mask of tingling warmth over his face, unaware that the first scenes of his life's incredible drama were unfolding in the valley below with the arrival in his village of two "strangers."

They reached Zapotitlán over an eight-hour trail from the "frontier" town of Zacapoaxtla, a trail that is celebrated as one of the worst in all Mexico. Mule drivers curse each step. The only time they stop is to gasp for the extra breath of air needed to pull themselves and their mules up the tortuous mud-soaked excuse for a road.

The tall skinny American, he with the shock of blond hair and the quick smile, was an instant novelty to the highland Totonacs. For many he was the first white man they had seen. The other turned out to be a stranger in dress only; he was a Christian Totonac, and this was his village.

The American rested against a stone fence and talked easily in Totonac with three young boys.

"My name is Mario," said one of the boys.

"And how are the other two called?" asked the American.

Mario, obviously the leader, pointed a dirty finger, "Oh, he is Pancho and he is Fulgencio." Fulgencio, a tall, fine featured youth, smiled shyly.

"How are you called?" the boys asked in chorus.

The American chuckled. "My name is Pedro. Pedro Aschmann."

"Don Pedro Aschmann," they repeated in unison. The words sounded strange coming from their mouths and they laughed—the laugh young boys laugh everywhere.

"Do you all live in the same house?" asked Herman.

"Not all of us," Mario cried. "Pancho and Fulgencio are the brothers of Vicente. There are four of us who play together."

"I see only three," questioned Aschmann.

"Our other friend," said Mario, "is just now coming down the trail. His name is Manuel."

Manuel joined his companions and listened as the stranger explained his reasons for coming to Zapotitlán. "How strange to wear shoes," he thought as he wiggled his bare toes in the dirt. "But stranger than wearing shoes is his wish to live in our village and learn the way we talk. He looks like a kind man—if I become his friend, I wonder if he would teach me about Mexico City."

At twenty-four, Herman Aschmann was the epitome of youthful optimism. "I'm going to Mexico as a Bible translator," he told his friends at Moody Bible Institute. During a chapel service, L. L. Legters, cofounder with William Cameron Townsend of the Wycliffe Bible Translators, impressed Herman with the fresh concept that linguistics and Bible translation were powerful evangelistic tools. Recently returned from Guatemala, Legters had seen the unusual results of Townsend's translation of the Cachiquel New Testament. He spoke of the many tribes in Mexico and thundered, "Not one of them has ever heard that freedom from sin comes from faith in Jesus Christ." Herman listened. He was impressed with the realism and love in Legters' voice, particularly when he spoke of reaching the Indians of Mexico in their own tongues. Herman decided he wanted to be a part of that team.

After a year and a half helping in that work with another tribe, Herman headed for the Totonacs. For two days he traveled 150 miles over an ancient narrow-gauge railway. Sore and stiff from the hard wooden seats, he detrained at the noisy hydroelectric town of Necaxa. From there he started inland to San Felipe Tecpatlan, a tiny Totonac village nesting on the side of a thickly forested mountain 3,000 feet above sea level. He arrived three days later, cold, wet and tired.

"Is there a place where I can sleep?" he asked, shivering in his rain-soaked jacket.

"You can sleep in here," said a short, dumpy man, proud to display his little-used mountain Spanish. Exhausted, Herman flopped on the rough, hand-hewn planks and drifted into a delicious sleep. Not until morning did he realize his host was the local bartender and he had slept in the back room of the town saloon!

With a broad grin Herman recalled later that he didn't really mind the saloon. It was just that he knew the sound of drunks falling on the floor would disturb his language studies. The only other available room in San Felipe was the town jail. Herman moved in. Unfortunately, he was never invited into the lives of the unfriendly and mildly hostile Totonacs in San Felipe. Fear and suspicion caused them to reject Herman with icy indifference.

Weeks led into months and not once was Herman able to persuade anyone to help him learn Totonac. Day after day he sat alone in the market square, listening with unbelieving ears to long tonal sounding words falling effortlessly from passersby. Occasionally he would catch an isolated word and write it down. The Totonac word for "good-by" almost made him weep. How would he ever learn to wrap his tongue around *nachuhuinampalayachowamaktum?*

After six frustrating months, Herman left San Felipe with his facility in Totonac as weak as his malaria-ridden body. To regain his strength and pursue his study of Totonac, he visited Townsend's village of Tetelcingo. There he found the solution to his language problem: Vicente Cortes, a bright, vibrant Christian Totonac who was Townsend's gardener. Months before, Vicente had come to Tetelcingo as a language helper for Landis and Jerdice

Christiansen, former Wycliffe translators who had been forced to leave Mexico because of ill health.

"If you want to speak Totonac," said Vicente to Herman one day, "why not come to my village. You can live in my house and I will teach you how to speak my language. The village is called Zapotitlán."

"I have lived in your village for twelve months," said Herman one day to Vicente, "now I must leave."

"Leave?" asked Vicente. "Why? My family are believers. My brother, Fulgencio, comes each day to study with you. There are fifteen to twenty young men who also come to study God's Word. Why would you want to leave our village so soon?"

Herman laughed. "I am not leaving forever, just a few months," he said. "It's just—well—the next time you see me I will have a wife."

"Oh!" said Vicente with a shy smile. "That is different!"

And it was different. After Herman returned with Bessie, his attractive bride, their house became the village bright spot. Within a week the Totonacs of Zapotitlán knew every detail of the Aschmann routine. Children stood in groups at each paneless window and amused themselves with the unfolding of the Aschmann's daily life. "How odd they are," they would say to their parents and friends. "The *señora* stands to cook." Then their eyes wide with the horror of the telling, they explained that she sat down and ate at the same time as the *señor.* "But what is strangest of all," they said, "is the way they close their eyes before eating their food!"

Manuel took his place with the others at the windows and watched. "It is true that they are different," he told his mother. "I never hear angry words from Señor Aschmann, nor do I see him hit his *señora* with the machete." Then with a shy smile on his face he added, "Sometimes the *señora* gives me candy and corn bread. But I wish Don Pedro had chosen me to help him learn our language instead of Fulgencio."

"Well," said Luz, "if you like them and they like you, just visit them and maybe one day he will ask you."

That day, inevitable as it later appeared, was brought closer by Fulgencio's accident, which occurred one day when Manuel was at a window of the Aschmann's house. Herman was seated at a desk of packing boxes, his bony fingers flying across the keys of a battered typewriter. On the back of the desk were commentaries, exegetical aids, and New Testaments in Spanish, Greek and English. Manuel watched and sighed, wishing he could understand those books. "Then I could be like Señor Aschmann and know everything!"

"Ah, Manuel," cried Herman in a quick, good-natured voice. "Come in and sit with me. I am trying to put the words of Jesus into your Totonac language. Would you like to hear how it sounds?"

Before Manuel could answer, the voice of Fulgencio's mother pierced the air. "Don Pedro! Don Pedro!" she cried. "I've killed my son! I've killed my son!"

Herman and Bessie rushed to the door and brought the small Totonac woman into their house. "Tell us what happened," said Bessie tenderly.

Her face twisted with grief and in a voice filled with distress, the mother told how Fulgencio slipped from the edge of the cornfield and fell many meters onto the rocks below. "Oh, Don Pedro," she wailed, "it was I who killed him because I insisted he go to the cornfield this morning when he wanted to work with you. Can you please come with medicines?"

For three desperate days, Bessie worked to stop Fulgencio's internal bleeding. When she failed, the village priest suggested oil and vinegar as a "sure cure." This nauseating mixture immediately produced violent vomiting, and Fulgencio died.

Almost immediately the church bells announced the event to the village, and Fulgencio's body was wrapped in a straw mat for burial. At the wake, Manuel listened and watched in amazed silence. Never before had the village of Zapotitlán experienced a Christian funeral. In a beautiful soprano voice, Bessie sang newly translated Totonac hymns. Vicente read passages of Scripture in Totonac.

A woman of another faith, impressed with this different approach to a funeral, was heard to say, "I see those gringos believe in God after all!" At the burial there were tears and the wailing of women. Friends and relatives covered the grave with the traditional *xaxanatnin,* the yellow flower of death.

Manuel lingered for a long time beside the grave. Staring into space, he let the yellow marigold petals flutter from his fingers. "What is it?" he thought, "What is it that Don Pedro and his *señora* have. How can they smile through tears when a person becomes buried?"

4

Words of Faith

"Don Pedro is like no other man in the village," said Manuel to Pancho one day.

"How is he different?" asked Pancho. "I don't see any difference."

"Oh, yes, there is a great difference," Manuel countered. "We both know our fathers enter each night to our houses drunk. Don Pedro never drinks. We know that when our fathers drink they curse and beat our mothers. Don Pedro never curses."

"Yes," said Pancho. "I've seen that he never hits his *señora.*"

"Have you noticed also that he loves each one that comes to his house?"

"No, I haven't."

"Well," said Manuel, "he does. When Old John, the one with burro's brains comes to his house, Don Pedro always takes time to talk with him. Don Pedro never laughs or tells stories about him like our fathers."

"One thing I heard," said Pancho, "he never cheats.

People of the village say when he sells medicine he always gives money back."

"But what is most different of all, and this I don't understand," said Manuel quizzically, "is that he talks very nice about the God he cannot see."

"How is that different?" questioned Pancho.

"His prayers," said Manuel slowly, "are not just recited from memory the way we do to our wooden gods."

"That is different," said Pancho. Then he added with a laugh, "But how foolish to pray to a God you cannot see."

"I agree," said Manuel thoughtfully. "But when I listen to him talk to his God he speaks words that come from his heart. Always to me they sound like Don Pedro is talking to a friend. And I want to know more about that."

It was shortly after this conversation that Herman spoke to Manuel about taking Fulgencio's place. Manuel's smile was warm and spontaneous as he listened to Don Pedro's unbelievable words. "I wonder if you would study with me like Fulgencio. I need someone to help me translate the Word of God into your language. As you help me I could teach you to read and write your own language. And you could learn about life beyond your mountain." Herman paused and waited for Manuel to speak.

Manuel, almost bursting, wanted to explain to this wonderful man that he had dreamed of nothing else since that first day he saw him in the village.

"Well, Manuel, what do you say? I will pay you to work for me like Fulgencio did."

"Oh, Señor Aschmann, to work and learn from you is my honor. It would not be right for me to take money just to teach you my language!"

In the weeks that followed, Herman and Manuel faced each other across a wooden table, and they made an unusual translation team. Herman's single-minded purpose to give the Scriptures to the Totonacs fired the boy's inquiring mind.

Manuel quickly understood the concepts of Bible translation, but he found it difficult to grasp abstract concepts of Scripture. "I can't see this faith, or smell it, or taste it," he would tell Herman. "If you could show me this, then maybe I would believe." In spite of his outward confusion, Manuel knew something was happening inside. The words of Scripture occupied his thoughts like molten silver dripping into his mind. The Scripture Herman read often triggered a provocative and pensive response.

"Is this truth?" said Manuel one day when Herman read Mark 1:27.

"Is what truth?"

"The words that Jesus is stronger than all the evil spirits."

"Yes," said Herman. "It is a true word. Why do you ask?"

Manuel thought for a moment and then said, "We Totonacs believe that when the sun falls behind our mountain, evil spirits fly in the air. And the only way to keep from being marked for death is to stay in our huts. This is why I never come to your house at night."

"Is death the only evil spirit that comes at night?"

"Oh, no!" said Manuel, his black eyes wide with fear. "The evil spirit that sucks life from children that are sick comes at night. Also the evil dwarfs of the forest." Anticipating Herman's questioning eyes, Manuel continued.

"The only way evil spirits leave sick people is when the *curandero* comes."

"What does he do?" asked Herman.

"First he looks at the person who is sick. Then he tells the father that for three days' wages in the cornfield, he will make the spirit leave."

"How does he make the spirit leave?"

"Come," said Manuel. "I can show you better than I can tell you." Manuel led Herman down a mud path, past crooked split-cedar huts that sagged under their heavy thick straw roofs. Manuel stopped in front of one of these huts. Herman recognized it as the hut Bessie had told him about earlier. She suspected the girl had malaria.

Manuel and Herman stood outside the door and called a greeting in Totonac. Immediately a voice from inside answered and invited them to enter. Herman bent his six-foot frame to four-and-a-half feet and passed through the small door. It was dark and smokey and smelled of burning pitch pine. As Herman's eyes adjusted to the darkness he noticed in one corner a small girl lying on a dirty straw mat. At her head were two gourds smoking like miniature smudge pots.

"How old is she?" he whispered to Manuel.

"She has ten years."

Herman didn't think that was possible. Why, the child couldn't be more than six! As he approached he noticed her normally burnished bronze face was the color of dull yellow custard. It was difficult for Herman to observe more because hovering over her like an eagle ready to strike, was the *curandero.*

With slow, deliberate movements he passed over the still form a bowl full of the blood of a freshly killed chicken. In low moaning chants, he asked the evil spirits to leave the body of the sick girl. After three or four chants the medicine man would stop to gulp a generous swig of corn liquor. Manuel whispered to Herman that this was part of the curing ritual. Herman also noticed the coagulated heart of a chicken at the foot of the wooden idols. After some minutes Manuel suggested to Herman that it was getting dark and he would have to go home. Herman offered his help to the girl's parents. When they refused, Herman excused himself and stepped outside.

"How is it that you know so much about the *curandero* and the evil spirits?" asked Herman when they were out of ear range of the hut.

There was a twinge of anger and sadness mixed in Manuel's voice as he spoke. "Not long ago the evil spirits sucked life from my brother's body. Each time the *curandero* came he would sacrifice one of my mother's chickens. Then he would say to my mother, 'Your son will be all right soon.' Then my mother would pay him money. It wasn't long before all our turkeys and chickens were gone. You know, Señor Aschmann, our turkeys are what we Totonacs sell for money. When they were gone, my mother borrowed money to buy more liquor and chickens for the *curandero.* All the time my mother prayed to the wooden masters to send the evil spirits away. But the evil spirits were too strong and he died. My mother then borrowed money for the fiesta of burial."

"Fiesta of burial?" questioned Herman.

"Yes, to keep the power of demons from my brother's soul, my mother bought candles, food and liquor for all that came."

"Well, how did your mother pay back the money she borrowed?"

"Oh," said Manuel. "That is sad. As an inheritance, my grandmother gave my mother a beautiful piece of land with coffee and all kinds of fruit trees. A Mexican man offered my mother a hundred pesos for it and she sold it to him. Often my mother cries for that land because she loved it deeply. And because now she knows the Mexican man cheated her. When I asked her why she sold it she said it was because she was an ignorant Totonac and there was no one to guide her. She told me that if I had gone to school that I could have helped her. She could have sold the land for at least a thousand *pesos.*"

"I'm sorry," said Herman after a long pause. Then added thoughtfully, "Do you remember the Scripture we read earlier this afternoon that said Jesus was stronger than the evil spirits?"

"Yes," said Manuel quietly.

"Well, do you know what that means?"

"No," said Manuel sheepishly, "I do not."

"It means that Jesus Christ is stronger than dwarfs of the forest, evil spirits of the night and those that suck life from children. It also means that He is stronger than even death."

"Stronger than death?" questioned Manuel.

"Yes," said Herman. "God promised that every person who would believe in His Son would have life forever. God also promised that if a person believed, Jesus would become his personal friend. He would never leave him. He also promised He would give that person courage not to be afraid of evil spirits wherever he went."

"The words you speak, Don Pedro, are beautiful. But I

have always believed that our wooden masters help us."

At the door of the Aschmann house Herman gave Manuel a friendly pat on the back and thanked him for the visit to the sick child.

"The honor is always mine," said Manuel politely. Then added, "I will work again on the day after tomorrow because tomorrow I must work in the cornfield."

With quick, even strokes Manuel cut into the tangle of green weeds growing between the young corn stalks. Since before dawn, he, his father and two brothers had worked without talking. Manuel was glad for the silence. It gave him time to think about Herman's words of the night before.

"They are so beautiful and they comfort me," he thought, "but it is hard for me to understand who is right. My mother, who tells me that the idols are the masters, or Señor Aschmann, who tells me there is one God and by this strange thing called faith He can live with me. Oh so many things to know and I know so little!"

It had been cold when Manuel started work. Now the big Mexican sun covered the mountainside cornfield like a great electric blanket. Manuel paused, lifted his sombrero and with the back of his hand wiped the perspiration from his forehead. For a moment he leaned on the end of his hoe and watched the bent figures of his father and brothers.

"How long," he thought, "will Totonacs cultivate the big cornfields for educated Mexicans. The educated people are the ones who own the land and send their children to school." "Hey!" called Manuel's father. "We of the Arenas family are paid to work, not dream!"

"Yes, Papa," said Manuel and automatically began chopping the weeds.

At the end of the day, Manuel went to the secret place in his backyard and carefully laid his wages for that day in the jug. Like all Totonacs, he believed that the only way to save money was to bury it. "When the pot is full," he said, recovering it with earth, "I will go to school in Mexico City!"

"Now," he said as he clapped his hands together to knock off the loose earth, "I will see if the gods of my mother will bleed."

5

Wooden Masters

Manuel picked out a long needle from his mother's sewing basket and slowly walked to a low shelf where his mother's sacred idols rested in dusty silence. Trembling, he reached out to touch the largest. Before his hands reached the gray forbidding figure he snapped them back to his side. He swallowed hard and ran his tongue across his dry lips. "I must find out if this god is real," he said aloud. "If I stick this needle into its foot and blood comes out, I'll know my mother is right. If it doesn't, I will know Don Pedro is right, and I will follow his God."

Great beads of perspiration stood out on Manuel's forehead as he took the idol from the shelf. With a quick thrust, he jabbed the needle into its foot. The needle snapped into pieces. He wiped his hand across the base of the idol's foot. There was only dust.

The color drained from Luz's face when Manuel told her what he had done. "Why did you do this?" she demanded.

"I'm trying to find the true God," said Manuel simply, "and I had to test my faith in these idols."

"What do you mean," said Luz angrily, "trying to find God! The masters on our shelves are real gods. It is a sin to call them idols. Now because of what you have done you will die in thirty minutes!"

The boy's heart sank. In his mind he was convinced the wooden masters were without spiritual significance or power. But his emotions were strongly tied to thirteen years of instruction by Luz.

"I will not die, little Mother," said Manuel trying to control his apprehension. "Don Pedro has told me the true God in heaven gives everlasting life to any person who believes in His Son. I will ask Don Pedro if he believes I will die in thirty minutes."

At the Aschmann's were five American visitors. One of these was Jack Wyrtzen, a youth evangelist from New York and founder of Word of Life Crusade. After the customary introduction, Herman noticed Manuel was unusually serious. Herman questioned him and the boy explained what he had done. Then he asked Herman hesitantly if he was sure the words he spoke on the trail were true.

In a quiet, sincere voice, Herman assured Manuel that God could not lie and that his words were true. Jack Wyrtzen sensed the boy's spiritual conflict and asked to speak to him, if Herman would interpret. Even though the intimacy of Herman and Manuel's conversation was broken, Manuel immediately felt Jack Wyrtzen's unusual warmth and concern for him as a person. As the evangelist explained the captivating truths of John 3:16, Manuel suddenly realized that this stranger, as had Don Pedro, was introducing him to a Person, that this Person was God and that God's love was directed at him personally. Like the morning sun that burns away the blue-gray mist to reveal a lush, green valley, Manuel met Christ in a golden moment of understanding.

When Manuel returned to his hut he found his mother weeping silently in front of her idols. "Little Mother," he said with a broad smile, "I have returned alive and well. You predicted death. Instead, I have been given life!"

At first, Manuel did not fully understand the significance of following Christ, but he knew immediately he would be unable to continue the family tradition of praying to wooden idols. Manuel's father stood it for a week. Then, true to his nature, he confronted Manuel with the thoughts that had been seething in his mind for months.

"My son," he said as Manuel prepared to leave for the cornfield one morning, "you are no longer fit to live in my house. Since your friend Don Pedro came to Zapotitlán you spend each spare hour in his house. You neglect your duties to my cornfield and the work you do for others. When I ask you why, you speak of this foolish notion of going to school in Mexico City. Not only do I listen to you babble like a burro, but my friends accuse me of having a traitor for a son. They tell me when you teach Don Pedro our language he sells the knowledge and becomes rich."

Manuel opened his mouth to speak but Mariano raised his hand to silence him. He continued, "Do you know why we have too much rain this year? Why our corn rots in the ground? It is because Don Pedro has disturbed and angered the ancient gods you refuse to worship."

"How has Don Pedro done this?" questioned Manuel, trembling.

"Whenever a Totonac refuses to worship the gods, like the people who call themselves Evangelicals—and like you, our valley suffers. St. Michael, who controls the thunder, will draw his sword and send blankets of rain to wash away our cornfields. Children will die because evil spirits will suck away their life. All this, my son, because Don Pedro has introduced a new religion to the Totonacs."

"No Papa," Manuel cried. "Not a new religion. Don Pedro only wants us to meet Jesus Christ. He is a Person. If you believe in your heart that He loves you then He can give you courage never again to be afraid of evil spirits."

"Enough," said Mariano angrily, "or you will feel the sting of my tumpline. You have only thirteen years and already you have disgraced my house. If you continue in this new way you will end up for the buzzards to pick your bones. Never forget that two Totonac Evangelicals were killed for preaching in the new church house that Don Pedro and his Evangelicals go to on Sunday. The whole village talks and laughs about my son Manuel."

"Why do they talk and laugh about me?" asked Manuel quietly.

"They say you are now too good to work in the cornfields like other Totonacs. Now, my son, I give you thirty minutes to make up your mind."

"Make up my mind on what, Papa?"

"Give up the foolishness of this new religion, worship the master gods with your mother and work in the cornfields with me. If you do not, you will leave this house immediately and take nothing with you. I will burn your books and the clothes your mother has made for the Fiesta of the New Year."

Manuel looked into his father's unsmiling face. The eyes

were half closed, chilling in their cold fury. The mouth was drawn tight over clenched teeth. Two fists were clenched and menacing. Manuel saw that his father trembled.

"Papa," pleaded Manuel, "how can I give up God, when He lives in my heart? Don Pedro's words are not false. He told me that Jesus Christ would give me courage against the evil spirits. For the first time since I can remember I am no longer afraid of the evil spirits of death when I am out in the darkness of night."

"I told you," said Mariano in a hoarse whisper, "that you have thirty minutes. Now you have fifteen!"

"Before you go," shouted Mariano as the boy shuffled slowly out of the hut and down the trail, "I will tell you one more thing. When you come to the fork in the trail, stop and think of what I have told you. If you take the left fork to Don Pedro's, you are forever lost to this house. You will no longer be my son!"

Manuel paused for a long time at the fork, looking in each direction, then turned left. With no other place open to him, Manuel presented himself at the Aschmann door. Herman, sensitive to Manuel's needs and deeply concerned with the unhappy turn of events, opened his home with the warmth and love of a devoted father.

For a year Manuel and Herman continued to work on translation. At first the steps were slow and painful, but together they walked deeper into the soul of the Totonac language. Each step was like opening a door into a dimly lit courtyard. As Herman passed through one, he found yet another to be opened. With each succeeding door, the courtyards appeared brighter until almost without knowing it the long Totonac words tumbled from Herman's lips as effortlessly as from any Totonac.

There were still concepts in Totonac that baffled him. In the beginning Herman wondered if he would ever understand the categories for counting.

"If you want to count men," Manuel would say, "then you say *chaʔtum,* which means one man; *chaʔtuy,* two men; *kalhaʔtut,* three men; or *kalhaʔtati,* four men.

"But," said Manuel with a sly smile, "if you wish to count something like a pencil or small round sticks, then you have to say *kanʔtum,* which means one thing round; *kanʔtuy,* two things round; or *kanʔtut,* three things round, and so on.

"Now if you want to count flat things like paper, then you say *pakʔtum,* which means one thing flat; *pakʔtuy,* two things flat; or *pakʔtut,* three things flat.

"And if you count things that are thick and flat like a book, then you say *macʔtum,* one thing flat and thick; *macʔtuy,* two things flat and thick; or *macʔtut,* three things flat and thick."

There were also problems in voice levels in Totonac that made Herman weep and Manuel laugh. *Chaʔn* with a catch in the throat over the "a" meant "to plant." *Chan* with no inflection means "ants." *Chān* with a mid-tone over the "a" meant "to arrive."

"Why would you want to hear Totonac stories?" asked Manuel when Herman asked him to tell one.

"Stories really help me to understand how your language works," answered Herman.

"Well," said Manuel, "my favorite is the story of the Rat's daughter."

Once upon a time there was a colony of rats that lived under a big rock. It is said one of them was a young lady eligible for marriage. She already had picked the one she wanted to marry although her father was against it. Papa Rat would not give his consent. "You aren't going to marry just anyone. You are going to marry the most important one in the world and I am going to find the one you are going to marry."

Papa Rat thought the Sun was the most important, so early in the morning he started out and climbed to the very top of a hill, waiting there until the Sun came out. "What do you want, my dear friend?" asked the Sun. "What can I do for you?"

"I have come to offer you the hand of my daughter. I want you to marry her because you are the most important person in the world."

The Sun laughed until his sides nearly split. "I am not the most important person in the world. The Cloud is. When he hides me from view, I can't shine any more. Talk to him."

"All right," Papa Rat said. And with that he turned around and scurried down the hill. He went to another big hill where all the Clouds gathered together. Papa Rat hadn't reached the top of the hill when the biggest Cloud spoke. "Where are you going, my dear friend?" he said.

"I am coming to you. I want to offer you the hand of my daughter. The Sun told me that you are the most important so I am coming to you. That is why I have come. I want you to accept my offer," the Rat replied.

"Poor you, my dear friend. I am not the most important," said the Cloud. "When I want to stay in one place, I can't. The Wind carries me far away. He carries me wherever he wants and I can't stay in one place. Talk to him."

"All right," said Papa Rat. So he went straight to where the Wind was and climbed a high hill. Before he even got all the way to the top, he began to shout to the Wind who was making a lot of noise as he blew. "Brother, I am coming," yelled Papa Rat.

"What do you want, my dear friend? What's on your mind?" asked the Wind.

So Papa Rat told him. "I have come to offer you the hand of my daughter. I want her to marry the most powerful one in the whole world. I believe that you are he because the Cloud told me so. I trust you will accept what I have come to offer."

"Poor you, my brother. I am not the one," said the Wind. "When I try to knock down a wall, I can't do it even though I try hard. Talk to the Rat. He can knock that wall down. He can get under it where I can't. He can scratch the dirt out from under the wall and that way he can certainly knock the wall down and I could never knock it down."

"All right," said Papa Rat, and he returned home without what he had been so determined to get. In the meantime, since the wind said the Rat was the greatest in the world, the young Lady Rat was overjoyed and she married the one to whom she had already given her heart.

When the story was finished, Manuel and Herman laughed together as good friends laugh. But to Herman the story was more than a primitive folk tale. It was a beginning treasure of important anthropological data and linguistic know-how. The natural flow of Totonac syntax in Manuel's story equipped Herman to translate the Scriptures with the same force of language that Christ used on

Palestinian ears. Herman knew stilted, wooden literalism in a translation could never adequately convey the power of Christ's words to the Totonacs.

"Our Totonac New Testament," he would say to Manuel, "must sound like Christ knows how to speak Totonac. And you, Manuel, are making this possible."

It took Manuel twelve months to save twelve Mexican dollars, a sum he earned by blistering his hands chopping firewood and clearing weeds from cornfields. On that day, after counting the coins in his savings jug twice, he announced to Herman that he now had enough to begin his education in Mexico City.

6

On Fire for the Lord!

The clock in the ancient cathedral tolled the evening hour of nine as the two policemen walked across the historic Zócalo in downtown Mexico City.

"How can an Indian boy who looks like he is only fifteen know any better?" said the first policeman.

"It makes no difference if he is an Indian or how old he is," argued the second. "The law forbids the giving out of Protestant religious papers."

"He must be very crazy or very brave to do it in front of the biggest cathedral in Mexico," said the first.

Oblivious to the approaching policemen, Manuel continued to press tracts into the hands of passersby. With each one he smiled, showing a set of strong white teeth.

"What are you doing here?" demanded the first policeman.

Manuel turned and looked at the blue-uniformed man. There was a sick feeling in his stomach as he whispered, "Just passing out tracts."

Enjoying his superiority and Manuel's obvious discomfort, the second policeman asked the boy if he knew that passing out religious papers was an offense against the law.

Manuel had been in Mexico City only a short time. At Herman Aschmann's suggestion he had been hired by George Cowan, the director of Wycliffe work in Mexico, to do odd jobs around the mission's headquarters. His Spanish lessons had not progressed very far, and now, confronted by the awesome presence of the law, he was struck dumb with fear unable to fully understand the unfamiliar Spanish words.

He managed a weak, "I did not know anything." While he was desperately seeking for words for an explanation in Spanish, a third policeman joined the other two. Out of the corner of his eye, Manuel saw him unclip the flap of his pistol holster. Nervously, Manuel opened his mouth, gave a thin smile and said, "I'm sorry——" He never finished. The third policeman swung his arm. Manuel saw a blue blur and felt the cold barrel of a pistol smash into his mouth. There was a cracking sound like a dry branch snapping under the weight of a heavy footfall. Manuel's mouth filled with warm blood. Then blackness.

Slowly Manuel opened his eyes, rolled them from side to side and blinked. He saw flowers, women dressed in white and lights brighter than a hundred lanterns. From somewhere out of sight the sound of soft music reached him. "I'm in a dream, or in heaven," he thought. "Never have I seen anything as beautiful as this."

Manuel wanted to explore further but he was pulled back into sleep by the magic of sedation. Before he fully surrendered he heard a voice say it was three in the morning and that a poor boy had slept five hours. When the sedation finally released him to consciousness, he knew the bubble of the earlier dream had popped. The hard reality of life screamed from the throbbing pain in his mouth. Manuel reached up to touch his teeth. To his horror his fingers passed through a gaping hole in his upper gum. All four upper front teeth were missing!

"Good morning," said the smiling nurse. "How are you?"

Suddenly aware of his strange surroundings and of being very much alone, Manuel asked through tear-filled eyes, where he was and why his face was swollen.

"Don't you know?" asked the nurse.

"No," said Manuel trying to keep back the tears.

"Then wait just a little minute and I will bring the superior to talk to you."

The mother superior of the hospital was an ageless woman with a face that people immediately trusted. She leaned over to speak to Manuel, her large winged cap throwing a shadow over his bandaged face.

"How do you feel, my son?"

"Not so good," replied Manuel. "There is pain in my face and elbow."

"The nurse tells me you can't remember what happened last night," she said. "Is that true?"

"Yes, I remember only going to church, then some young people asked me to pass out tracts in the Zócalo and that's all. I remember nothing more."

"Don't you remember being hit in the face?" asked the mother superior.

"No," replied Manuel. "I remember nothing."

"I will explain everything later," she said kindly, "but first you must eat."

A nurse's aide laid a tray of strange food across his lap,

then left. Manuel gazed at the puzzling array of soft foods. "How could anyone think of eating a meal without *tortillas,* beans, and *panela* sweetened coffee?" he wondered. But then he reasoned, "How could I eat *tortillas* without front teeth!"

When Manuel failed to show up on Monday morning to perform his chores at mission headquarters, Herman Aschmann feared the worst. "He must be in trouble," he replied when George Cowan asked if he had seen the boy. Fortunately, Herman's first phone call was to the Red Cross ambulance service. To his amazement they remembered taking a young Indian boy to the Juarez Charity Hospital.

Herman handed the flowers he brought for Manuel to a nurse's aide and sat down beside his bandaged friend.

"If God can keep me from evil spirits," Manuel questioned Herman, "why didn't He keep me from evil men?"

"God keeps us from evil spirits when we protect ourselves with His Word. We do this when we memorize Scripture and keep it in our minds," said Herman. "It's like having a sharp machete to kill the evil spirits. Scripture also promises us that when we are doing what God wants us to do everything that happens to us works out for our good. At this moment it is hard for both of us to understand why God allowed a policeman to hurt you. We know that God has a plan for your life and maybe some good will come out of this."

"Manuel," continued Herman tenderly, "perhaps someone came to understand about Christ through the tracts you gave them last night, or maybe someone became stronger in his faith when he saw your courage. I know you're worried about your teeth, but I'll help you get new ones when you are feeling better."

Manuel met his formative school years in Mexico City with courage, humor and a strong determination to learn. Like a weaver designing a regional masterpiece, Manuel wove people, experiences, practical education, and academic life into the fabric of his personality. The pattern was a unique tapestry of pristine innocence, spiritual sensibility and worldly prudence. Even mechanical things, which still remained something of a mystery, he wove into his personality for a richer design.

On his first visit to a downtown office building, Manuel watched in amazed silence as Herman pushed a button on the elevator. Wide-eyed, Manuel saw the doors appear from nowhere and seal them in the "box." Herman pressed another button and Manuel felt his stomach rise as they were carried swiftly to the top floor. He thought this was the most wonderful experience of his entire life. Even more fun than riding a second-class bus!

Several days later Manuel returned to the same building. When he arrived, the elevator was open and empty. He stepped inside and pushed a button. To his great delight, the door closed. Manuel pushed another button but this time he went down instead of up. Not knowing what to do, he pushed another button. The elevator stopped and then started up. For thirty minutes Manuel tried in vain for the right combination of buttons that would stop the elevator and open its doors. He realized his difficulty stemmed from his inability to read the Spanish signs. By the time he was rescued by an attendant, he was determined that learning to read would be the first step in his education.

The little book made a slapping sound as it flopped on the washroom floor.

"Hey, what's this?" said Carlos bending down to pick it up.

Unsmiling, Manuel said, "Read it!"

Like most high school seniors, Manuel had enjoyed the weekly workout on the basketball court with his friends. Carlos Gonzalez, one of that ever-widening circle, had returned with him to the washroom to clean up. In pulling his handkerchief from his back pocket to dry his hands, Manuel had accidentally flicked out his New Testament.

"This is a nice little book," said Carlos. "What is it?"

"Yes," said Manuel with an impish smile, "it is. Read it."

Carlos wiped the palms of his hands on the front of his pants. Half expecting to read a juicy morsel, he opened to the first page and read, "Presented to Manuel Arenas by the First Presbyterian Church of Mexico City." He sniffled disdainfully, uttered a contemptuous, "Oh a Protestant book," and threw it back on the floor.

The two eighteen-year-old boys faced each other in silence. Carlos, taller by a head and thirty pounds heavier, waited for Manuel to speak.

With eyes and jaw set and in a firm, quiet voice, Manuel said, "Carlos, you offered to pick up my book. Then you said you would read it. You didn't tell me you would throw it away. Now, Carlos, what you have done is very bad. The book you threw on the floor is God's Word. You must respect this book because it is God's Word."

Never in all the four years Carlos had known him had Manuel acted so completely out of character. The students loved Manuel. His kind, sensitive personality attracted others to him naturally.

"Manuel," said Carlos, "I have never seen you angry with me before."

"That's true," said Manuel softly, "but now I am angry because what you have done is not right." Manuel paused and lowered his voice to almost a whisper. "Now, will you please pick up that Book and hand it to me."

"I'm sorry," said Carlos as he returned the New Testament.

Manuel looked at Carlos for a long moment, then said, "Carlos, it is one thing to say sorry with your mouth, but it is another thing to say sorry from the heart and really feel it. I'm glad you said you were sorry because if you are, you will listen to what I have to say."

"Yes," said Carlos, "I will listen."

Manuel began to explain to Carlos the importance of knowing Jesus Christ in a personal way.

"Oh," said Carlos. "I'm ashamed. I'm the one who should be a strong Christian, but I'm not. But I don't think a washroom is the proper place to discuss God. Come to my home on Saturday at noon for lunch and we can talk then."

Having a strong propensity for punctuality, Manuel actually arrived thirty minutes before the appointed hour. Believing it impolite to knock, he waited outside the front door which he noted was slightly open. While Manuel stood outside, he overheard Carlos giving detailed instructions to his younger brother, Armando.

"Listen, Armando. My friend Manuel is coming to talk

to me about his religion, which I hate. Two Sundays ago our priest told us about the Protestants and I don't like them. When Manuel comes, you tell him I am not here."

"But," said Armando weakly, "suppose he asks me where you are. What should I say?"

"Just tell him I went to town on urgent business. I will not be back for about four hours. When he hears that, he will go home and eat."

When Manuel heard this, he thought, "Oh, what a liar! What a liar!"

Promptly at twelve o'clock Manuel knocked at the door. Armando opened it but blocked the entry with his body.

"Oh," said Manuel cheerily. "Are you Armando?"

"Yes, I am."

"I am glad to meet you," said Manuel. "I have heard a lot about you."

"Thank you," said Armando. "You are Manuel?"

"Yes, I am."

"I suppose you want to see my brother, Carlos."

"Yes. We are to have lunch together."

"Well," answered Armando sheepishly, "you have come at the wrong time. Carlos had a phone call and had to go downtown right away. He said to tell you he is sorry to miss the appointment."

"That's too bad for me," said Manuel. "He knew I was coming at twelve."

"Well, that is one of those things that happen. You go back home and eat because it will be three or four hours before Carlos comes home."

"Three or four hours doesn't mean anything to me. I can wait," Manuel said as he pushed by Armando and walked into the house.

The room was empty except for two low-slung beds and a small desk between them. His mind burning with feverish curiosity, Manuel determined to locate Carlos. As he cast his eyes slowly around the room, he noticed movement of one of the bed covers. "Ah," he thought, "so that's where he is," and he sat down in the middle of the bed to wait. Armando tried to talk Manuel into playing outside with the dogs.

"No," said Manuel. "I will just wait here." And he did, for three uncomfortable hours. Once he said, "Armando, I hear noises under the bed."

"Oh," Armando called back, "don't pay any attention. It is just little cats playing there."

"Well," Manuel teased, "have compassion and take them outside because really they are making too much noise." Manuel had almost given up when it happened. Exhausted Carlos inched his way out from under the bed.

"Armando," said Manuel, "I want to show you something. Look at the little kitten. He is coming out from under the bed!"

"Oh yes," said Armando laughing. "It is a big cat." And all three laughed and laughed and laughed.

"Are you sorry again?" asked Manuel.

"I am more than sorry," said Carlos sadly. "I can't tell you how sorry I am for what I have done."

"I understand. I know all about it."

"How did you know?"

"I heard you talking outside," Manuel said simply.

"Oh," groaned Carlos. And he cried.

"Why do you cry?"

"Because," answered Carlos, "you no longer have confidence in me."

"No, no! I have not lost confidence in you. I am your friend. Maybe all this has happened because God wants to teach you a lesson. Listen, Carlos, I would like it if you would let me pray."

"Yes, please do."

"Lord," said Manuel softly, "forgive Carlos, because he did not know what he did. But I want him to be on Your side."

Carlos, moved by Manuel's honest concern for him, began to cry again, this time almost without control.

"I am glad you cry," said Manuel, "because you feel it in your heart. Do you want to accept the Lord? I will ask the Lord to forgive you but what God wants is that you will speak to the Lord and pray."

"But, Manuel, I don't know how to pray."

"If you want to accept the Lord," said Manuel, "I will teach you how. But before you do that, don't think I am forcing you."

"No," said Carlos. "I want to accept the Lord. It is my own will right now."

As Manuel later related the story of how Carlos came to know the Lord he would say enthusiastically, "Oh, I am telling you! I am telling you! Carlos is really on the fire for the Lord!"

But Carlos wasn't the only one on fire for the Lord. Even though his artificial teeth were a constant reminder of his painful ordeal, Manuel continued a bold, winsome witness wherever and whenever the opportunity.

One such opportunity occurred one afternoon on his return from playing the concertina for a small church on the outskirts of Mexico City. He noticed a large crowd in Chapultepec Park near his bus transfer point and, eternally curious, he walked over to the crowd to investigate. After watching the spectacle for a time it struck him that if a troupe of clowns throwing coins and gamboling about could get such an audience, maybe he could too. He walked a short distance from the crowd and making himself comfortable on a park bench, stretched his concertina to the limit and began to play gospel songs.

"Hallelujah, brother! Keep playing! We're praying for you," said two elderly ladies as they came to watch. Within minutes the ladies were joined by more than two hundred people, and Manuel, who knew better than anyone present that he was no preacher, nevertheless felt he had to speak for his Lord.

"How many of you know about the Virgin of Guadalupe?" he asked, knowing full well he was referring to Mexico's most revered saint. As he expected, every hand was raised, men doffed their hats, and with one excited voice his audience yelled, *"¡Viva la Virgin de Guadalupe!"*

"How many of you," he continued, "know about the Lord Jesus Christ? How He came to be born in this world and how He died and rose again?" Again every hand shot into the air.

"Now the third question I have," said Manuel, "is this. What was the purpose of Christ's death on the cross?" Manuel looked around at the crowd. No one raised his hand. Then he said pleasantly, "Would you like me to tell you?" Again with one voice the crowd answered, *"¡Sí, sí!"*

"A long time ago," said Manuel, "before Jesus was born, men sacrificed animals to take away their sins. But

God said the only way people could really have their sins taken away was if His Son, Jesus Christ, would come to earth and pay for those sins. That is why Christ died on the cross. God says that if we believe that Christ died for our sins we would have eternal life." Manuel was warming to his subject when he heard the explosive blast of several motorcycles. "Oh," groaned Manuel. "Police!"

Knowing arrest was inevitable if he was caught, Manuel dropped his concertina and started to run. "He is doing nothing!" said the crowd when the policemen demanded to know the reason for the gathering. "He is just explaining about the Lord Jesus Christ." Some young boys in the crowd immediately linked arms and tried to impede the policemen. The remainder of the crowd, sympathetic to Manuel and knowing the policemen's unorthodox methods of handling prisoners, began to jostle and block the officers in their attempt to chase Manuel.

"Quick!" said a voice. "Come with me!" To Manuel's surprise, a woman grabbed him by the arm. Together they ran to her car and in a moment were out of the park and to safety.

"I'll let you out in a few blocks," said the woman, "and you can take a bus to your home. If you give me your address, I'll go back to the park and see if I can get your concertina."

"Thank you," said Manuel. "That would be kind."

When Manuel reached Wycliffe headquarters, where the news of his encounter had preceded him, his friends wanted to know how he happened to lend his accordion to a beautiful lady!

"Well," said Manuel weakly, "I will tell you later."

7

"All I Want Is Sandwiches"

Both letters arrived at the same time. One, written on crisp, white bond in bold type, was clear and concise.

> Dear Mr. Arenas:
>
> It is my pleasure to inform you that upon recommendation of five prominent Mexican lawyers, you have been granted a General Electric scholarship to study Civil Engineering at the Massachusetts Institute of Technology.

It was signed by the director of admissions. Manuel laid the letter on the edge of his bed and wondered if his eyes betrayed him.

The second letter was faded and written on a typewriter badly in need of cleaning.

> My dear Manuel:
>
> You will be happy to know the church in Zapotitlán has grown to over five hundred. I am so happy to see

the Lord's great blessing, but I am also sad. I am sad because the New Testament is not finished and I am concerned that the church become weak. We both know its strength will come only from instruction by the Holy Spirit. But the Holy Spirit must work through God's Word.

Because of the many visitors and medical cases, I have decided to work on translation outside the village. But to do this I need your help. If I am to push ahead on translation, I need six months in Norman, Oklahoma. Could you join me there? I will pray for the Lord to guide you in your decision.

Your friend,
PEDRO

Manuel tossed the letter from Herman Aschmann on the bed with the first and gave a long sigh. "What am I to do?" he wondered. "I told the Lord I would use my education for Him. But how can I get an education if I spend the next six months working on translation?"

It took Manuel a long time to weigh the implications of the letters. The scholarship from M.I.T. seemed the complete fulfillment of all his dreams. "Besides assuring me of a well-paying job," he reasoned, "I can perfect my English, live in the States and serve the Lord better." But then he thought of the Totonacs and he knew his reasoning was hollow. "They are alone, afraid and full of superstition. They must understand, as I understand, that Jesus Christ forgives sin and gives new life." Deep down he knew this understanding could only come through the New Testament in Totonac. "I wonder how many days it takes to Oklahoma," he concluded.

The days in Oklahoma were filled with hard, intense work. Some days were painful. It was not uncommon for Herman and Manuel to spend three and four days on a single Scripture passage. Because there was no religious vocabulary in Totonac, words like "sanctification," "justification," "predestination," were particularly troublesome. Often Manuel wished he had a job at which he could work with his hands and never again have to use his head. These were his thoughts; but he never showed it, and Herman would later say of Manuel that he was the most astute Christian he had ever known.

"Instead of us pushing him for more hours," said Herman, "he would push us. He was absolutely untiring. His attitude was, 'Woe is me if I don't help finish the Totonac New Testament.' Without him we could never have done it."

From Oklahoma, Manuel bused to California to record a series of gospel records in Totonac. And then to polish the shine on his blossoming academic life, he returned to Mexico City to attend the International Business School. In addition to courses in typing, shorthand and bookkeeping, Manuel took an elective in etiquette and proper dress habits. Most people are surprised by his natty appearance!

After graduating at the business school in 1952, Manuel returned once more to the States with Herman, this time to Sulphur Springs, Arkansas. There the Totonac New Testament was completed, revised and prepared for publication. In the fall of that year Herman and Manuel traveled through Arkansas and Tennessee on official deputation for

Wycliffe Bible Translators. Naturally warm and vibrant, Manuel was an instant success as a public speaker.

"His humble, unpretentious personality just flows right through to his audience," said Ralph Hookaby, a retired preacher from Sulphur Springs, Arkansas.

"Yes," said another. "Even though Mr. Aschmann has to interpret from Totonac to English, I am aware of an uncommon sincerity. His relationship to Christ is obvious and beautiful. He makes me feel the importance of the New Testament in his own language to be all consuming."

It was at Bob Jones University in Greenville, S.C., that charisma flowed in both directions. After speaking in chapel and viewing the grounds and curriculum, Manuel knew instantly this was the place to begin his formal Bible study.

Ralph Hookaby overheard Manuel's conversation with Herman. "Since my good friend is the secretary of Bob Jones University," he said, "I just may be able to get Manuel a scholarship." And he was as good as his word. Within three weeks Manuel received a letter advising him that pending a sponsor, he would be enrolled in the fall of 1953 on full scholarship. Mr. Amos Baker from Tulsa, Oklahoma, a long-time friend and lay representative for Wycliffe, volunteered to be that sponsor. Almost beside himself with joy, Manuel returned to Mexico City to arrange for student visa papers.

Then it happened! Fevers and severe headache at first. Then for reasons unknown to Manuel, his nose began to bleed and he felt unusually weak. "Malaria," he thought. "My malaria is coming back."

But it wasn't malaria! After six days of muscle spasms and stupefying delirium, Manuel's condition was diagnosed as typhoid fever. For five days of the first four crucial weeks, Manuel's temperature burned at 103 to 104 degrees. With ice packs and alcoholic baths, Wycliffe nurse Florence Gerdel gradually brought the fever under control. The effects of the disease were severe enough to cause knowledgeable people to wonder if Manuel would live. But with medication, diet and prayer, Manuel began a six-month struggle to regain his normal health.

In addition to overcoming his physical ailment, Manuel also battled the despair of losing a scholarship at Bob Jones University. The due date for acceptance came in the middle of his convalescence. "I am very sad," he told his friends, "but I am thankful to the Lord for giving me back my health. And I am also thankful to the Lord that He gave me the scholarship to encourage me. But now I must say it wasn't the Lord's will for me to go there. Now I will go to my village for two months and do evangelistic work."

It was a small room with an uneven dirt floor. The rough, hand-split rock walls once the color of dull marble, were stained black from years of exposure to smoldering cooking fires. Sunlight from an open crevice that served as the only window, fell across Manuel's smiling face. His audience of about thirty Totonacs of both sexes sat silent and unsmiling.

"I just want to share my faith with you," he said. "I want to tell you how happy I am because Jesus Christ has released me from fear and has become my personal friend." He went on to explain in slow, deliberate fashion that wooden idols would never help them. "Because," he continued, "I have proved that they are not real. For many years I prayed to the gods. I said,

> You have given me long life.
> You have given me the best life.
> It is good life you have given me.
> Now I want to give the best I have to you.
> I can't give you my heart, so I give
> you the heart of this sacrificed bird.

"This prayer is the kind of prayer we should pray to the true God," continued Manuel, "but only if we would change it a little bit. Instead of giving a bird's heart, we can, in faith, give our own hearts. If we pray that prayer to the true God who is Jesus Christ, then we no longer have to pray to idols who do not hear and who cannot move."

During this talk, Manuel noticed small knots of men outside. They talked in excited voices and shook their fists in the direction of the small stone building. Manuel also noticed his friends in the church becoming visibly nervous. When the service was finished, Manuel was quickly rushed to a friend's house and there they made him change into Indian clothing.

"The people in this village did not like what you said about the gods," said his friend. "There are many who believe that corn will not grow and sickness will come if sacrifices are not made to the gods. The men standing outside were so angry that I heard them say that you should be killed. This is why you must wear Indian clothes and hide in my corn bin until a little while is passed."

Manuel hid in the corn bin for two hours while groups of angry villagers harassed the homes of known evangelicals. Fearful of his being discovered, Manuel's friends persuaded him it would be safer to leave the village by a back trail. But no sooner had Manuel left than two of his pursuers stopped him on the trail just outside the village. "Good afternoon, Uncle," they said. "We are looking for a foreigner. Have you seen him along the way?"

"No," Manuel answered, "I have seen no foreigner." Then, straightening himself to his full five feet four inches, he added, "but perhaps I am he."

"Oh, no," laughed the men. "How could you be the foreigner? You wear Indian clothes and speak Totonac. The man we are looking for speaks Spanish and wears clothes from the outside." They smiled at each other and walked away. Manuel smiled to himself and walked out to safety.

Manuel reached Mexico City with 175 pesos in his pocket, 100 of which would be needed for the one-way ticket to El Paso, Texas. When his friend Benjamin, with whom he had boarded through high school, discovered Manuel's ridiculous sum, he offered to loan him extra money.

"No," said Manuel, "all I want is sandwiches. Will you ask your mother to make enough sandwiches for my trip to the border."

"No," said Benny, visibly angry, "they will spoil. Just tell me how much money you want and I will give it to you."

"Listen, Benny," said Manuel firmly, "if I wanted money, I would have asked for it. All I want is sandwiches."

"All right," said Benny with a sigh of defeat. "How many do you think you will need?"

Manuel had one sandwich left when he walked into the customs building at the border. However, the officers were not concerned about the condition of his larder.

"How much money do you have?" asked the American border official.

Manuel reached into his pocket and pulled out his wallet. With careful, measured movements, he slowly counted his money. Looking up into the face of the tall Texan, Manuel announced cheerily that he had seventy-five.

"Seventy-five pesos, or seventy-five dollars?" questioned the official.

"Pesos," said Manuel weakly.

"You mean all you have is the equivalent of six American dollars?" asked the official.

Manuel smiled brightly and nodded.

"Well, young man," said the official, trying hard to be firm and unfriendly, "I'm sorry but I can't let you cross into the United States with only six dollars. Come back when you have three hundred."

Crushed, Manuel walked back across the border into the narrow congested streets of Ciudad Juarez. "Above all things," he thought, "I have dreamed of getting my education in English. I wanted to go to Biola for my training. What is the Lord trying to teach me?"

"Manuel! Manuel!" cried a voice. "What are you doing here in Juarez?"

Manuel pushed his thoughts from his mind and looked up into the smiling face of a woman.

"You remember me," she said. "I am the aunt of Carlos and Armando!"

"I am sorry," she said, when Manuel told her his story. "But," she continued thoughtfully, "Armando is now a pilot, and he is at this moment at the airport on the Mexican side. I am sure he will help."

Armando was eager to help his old friend. "Is three hundred dollars all you need?" he asked jokingly.

"That is all," said Manuel with a weak smile and a long sigh.

Without realizing what was happening, Manuel saw Armando reach into his pocket and pull out a checkbook.

"Here," said his friend. "See if this will get you past the border official."

The border official lifted his cap and scratched his head in unbelief as Manuel showed him that his six dollars had, in three hours, multiplied to four hundred!

8

Breakfast at Gaston's

The breakfast line in Gaston's Cafeteria in Dallas was long and slow-moving. As Manuel pulled his plastic tray along the shiny chrome rack he looked around at the crowd and noticed the dark complexioned man smile at him from his nearby position in the line.

"Hello," said Manuel brightly. "I have seen you many times. Do you work close by?"

"Yes," said the young man. "I am a doctor from Baylor Medical School."

"How nice," said Manuel. "And what part of Latin America are you from?"

The man's mouth broke into a bright, full smile below his black mustache. "Why do you ask if I am from Latin America?"

"Because," said Manuel, "you are brown."

"I am sorry to disappoint you," said the doctor with a laugh, "but I am not from Latin America. My name is Karzzin Kurtartt and I am from Turkey."

"Oh," said Manuel excitedly, "I am so glad to meet you. I have never met anyone from Turkey before. My name is

Manuel Arenas and I am from Mexico. Won't you have breakfast with me."

Neither man realized then the depth to which their friendship would grow in the weeks that followed. The young doctor, a devout Moslem, found it difficult at first to understand Manuel's reasons for attending Bible school. The son of a wealthy family, he was more bewildered by Manuel's bizarre explanation of how he came to Dallas College.

"I wanted to study at Biola College in California but I arrived too late in the year to enroll. I thought I would just work and wait for the next year, but some American friends encouraged me to attend Prairie Bible Institute in Canada. The idea sounded good and I went. After a year at Prairie, I returned to Mexico. It was my plan to return in the fall but I got sick for a second time with typhoid fever. The money I saved for tuition working on a construction gang in Canada, I spent in a hospital bed in Mexico. After I recovered, some friends offered to help me pay my tuition if I would continue with my education, so I decided to attend Moody Bible Institute in Chicago."

"It seems to me," said Kurtartt with a smile, "you play with schools like a child plays with a new toy."

"You think so?" asked Manuel innocently.

"Please continue," said his Turkish friend. "All this fascinates me."

"I took a bus to Dallas on my way to Chicago. In Dallas I had to change buses and because I had a couple of hours to wait, I decided to walk in the streets. I came to the Dallas Rescue Mission and from the street I heard nice voices singing. So I walked inside and saw a group of students. 'What kind of students are you?' I asked. They said they were from Dallas College. When I told them I was going to Moody Bible Institute, one of the students asked me to come back with him. In the morning I went to chapel and was impressed with the students and the intimacy of the school. I said to myself, 'This is the school for me!' For the past three years I have worked nights and go to school there in the day. I will graduate in the spring."

"Very interesting," said Kurtartt, "but very different. I want to hear about your faith sometime."

Manuel smiled and said, "You will!"

But Manuel knew that before he could share his Christian experience in a meaningful way, he would first have to win Kurtartt's confidence. Early in their association Manuel discovered that his Turkish friend possessed a brilliant mind. "It would be useless to discuss anything with him yet," he told himself. "I would be no match for Kurtartt and besides I know nothing about Islam."

He began his campaign innocently enough by inviting Kurtartt to a get-together of a few foreign students from S.M.U. and Arlington State College at the home of a Christian doctor friend of his.

"Fine," said Kurtartt, "I would very much like to meet your friends—but remember, I am Moslem."

Manuel's more conservative friends felt at first that Manuel was indifferent to Kurtartt's spiritual need. Once when Manuel and he attended the First Baptist Church in Dallas, some energetic people urged Kurtartt to become a Christian.

"Look," said Kurtartt firmly to Manuel later, "I did not mind coming to church with you, but the next time you invite me to a meeting, will you please tell these people not to press me about their religion. Just tell them I am a Moslem."

So on the next occasion, to friends at the First Presbyterian Church in Dallas, it was "This is Dr. Karzzin Kurtartt, my Moslem friend." Kurtartt, his hands clasped behind him, rocked back on his heels, gave a short bow and smiled brightly, pleased with his friend's new approach.

During the Christmas vacation of 1958 Manuel again resorted to the device of exposure in his campaign to win his friend to Christ. This time he invited Kurtartt to spend the holidays in Shreveport, Louisiana, at the home of Mom and Pop Wagner.

"Who?" asked Kurtartt.

"The Wagners," said Manuel happily. "They are an older Christian couple who love young people and are very much interested in foreign students. So many students come to their house they number them."

"What number are you?"

"I," Manuel said proudly, "am Son 72!"

At prayer at the Wagner's it was the custom for all—Japanese, Norwegian, German, Italian, Chinese, Mexican and Turkish, often as many as eighteen students from as many countries—to sit with heads bowed. Pop Wagner led the prayers and daily thanked God for sending Jesus Christ to be the Saviour of the world. There were always other words such as "warm Christian fellowship," "safety for travel," and even "for sending Manuel and Kurtartt to spend Christmas in our home."

The words impressed the young doctor even though he didn't agree with some of them. He liked Pop Wagner and the way he spoke to God, sort of like he knew Him privately.

"Look, Manuel," said Kurtartt, one day, "I've been listening to you tell me about Christ. I have visited your Christian friends for a long time. Now I want to tell you some things. First, I want you to take my Koran and read it. Then I want you to tell me what you think about it. But first I must tell you I think the Koran is better than the Bible."

After he had read the Koran, Manuel told his friend there seemed to be one important difference between the two.

"What's that?" asked Kurtartt.

"First of all," said Manuel, "I like it. It is very nice. But the important difference is that Christ was not merely a prophet as the Koran says He was. Christ is the Son of God, the Saviour of the world. Now in the Koran there are a lot of parts that come from the Bible. If you know the history of the Bible, you know the Bible was written first. You also know that Mohammed was a businessman and in his travels he became acquainted with Christianity, so he formed the Islamic faith from the Bible." Manuel warmed to his subject and continued his religious reasoning with true Latin American exuberance.

"Now, if you do not believe my words," he concluded, "that's okay. But you must believe God's Word."

It wasn't the brilliance of Manuel's logic that impressed Kurtartt. It was Manuel's simple declaration that everyone has to obey God's Word, that there is absolutely no room for anything less than total commitment. Kurtartt smiled to himself and wondered how anyone could possibly be so sure that Christ was really a divine person and would give direction to an individual's life if a person asked Him.

"No one invited me to give a speech."

The room was suddenly silent, as though someone had flipped a switch and turned off all sound. Kurtartt was on his feet amid the seated participants of the foreign students' meeting.

"But since some of you gave your testimonies I, too, would like to say something. I have been to your meetings many times. You all know that I am Moslem. Well, tonight I want to say that because Manuel has always been kind and helpful and because he showed me friendship when he told me about your faith, I want to tell you now that I am half Baptist and half Moslem."

"That sounds good," thought Manuel, "but I wonder what he means. Does he think that because we have been attending mostly Baptist churches I am trying to make a Baptist out of him instead of a Christian?" The thought bothered Manuel but because of exams and then the phone call, he had no time to discuss its implications with his friend. The phone call came while he was at work.

"Hello, Manuel, this is Kurtartt speaking. I just called to tell you that I am leaving for Istanbul tonight at eleven."

Shocked, Manuel was barely able to answer.

"Why, Kurtartt? Why didn't you tell me sooner?" asked Manuel in a hoarse whisper.

"I am sorry," said Kurtartt, "but I received a telegram today advising me that my father is very ill. I have a stopover in New York but I must leave tonight to make connections to Istanbul."

Manuel knew Kurtartt did not fully understand the importance of a personal relationship to Jesus Christ. He also knew if he didn't speak to Kurtartt once more about accepting Christ there would never be another opportunity.

"I will leave my work and go with you to the airport," said Manuel.

"Good," answered Kurtartt. "I will look for you."

Manuel's heart sank. The apartment was full of people helping Kurtartt pack and dispose of last-minute details. "How can I speak to him with all these people here," Manuel wondered.

At the airport, Manuel was frustrated again. There were just too many who had come to wish Kurtartt farewell.

"I have a doctor friend doing graduate work at Columbia," said Manuel as he gave Kurtartt a Mexican *abrazo.* "I will call him to meet you and help you during your stopover in New York. His name is Carlos Gonzalez."

Manuel called Carlos upon his return from the airport.

"I am so happy to hear you," his old friend said. "You must have an important reason for calling long distance at this hour."

"Yes," answered Manuel, "I have a very important reason."

Quickly Manuel told Carlos of his relationship with Kurtartt and how close he felt Kurtartt was to becoming a Christian. "If you could meet him and take him to church I would be so happy."

Two days later Manuel received a letter from New York. "Who would write me from the Waldorf Astoria?" he wondered as he first fingered and then opened the heavy bond envelope.

My dear Manuel,

It is now 2:00 P.M. Dr. Carlos and I are eating here at the Waldorf Astoria. But I didn't write to tell you where I am eating. I have some good news for you. (Manuel's eyes filled with tears as he continued to read.) You will never know, my good friend, how very much I appreciated your love and kindness to me during this past year. Your friendship has meant more to me than all my father's wealth. Of all the people I have ever met, no one has ever shown me such wonderful friendship. I want to tell you that Dr. Carlos is like you also, very kind and considerate. He has helped me greatly this morning when I arrived in New York. Do you remember the last meeting when I told the people I was half Baptist and half Moslem? Well, Manuel, I want to tell you now that Dr. Carlos took me to church this morning, and when the pastor made the invitation, I was first to walk down the aisle. Now, Manuel, I want you to know that I am not half Baptist, half Moslem any more. I am full Christian!

Three weeks later Manuel received a second letter from Kurtartt. This time the postmark was Istanbul. In simple, direct words it read:

You will be happy to know, Manuel, through God's goodness my father, my brother, and my sister have come to know the Lord. Pray for us all that we will be strong in our new faith. There are rumblings that the authorities do not like what I do and I might be put in jail. [Manuel later learned that Kurtartt was indeed jailed but was subsequently released because the government needed his medical skills.] The Turkish authorities believe that anyone who speaks out for his faith must be Communist. There is religious freedom here but Christians are treated like your Negroes in the States, sort of second-class citizens.

Not all Manuel's contacts remembered him as fondly as Kurtartt and Carlos did. It was the summer after Dallas, and Manuel was waiting while the Guatemala customs official typed up his visa. Apparently it was the English edition of *Life* magazine tucked under his arm that prompted the question from the man standing before him. "Do you speak English?"

"Yes," said Manuel politely, "I do."

"May I sit beside you?"

"Yes," smiled Manuel. "Please do."

"Thank you," said the man. "Oh," he said as an afterthought, "this is my wife." He continued, "I'm an American evangelist and am scheduled to hold a week of meetings in Guatemala City. Unfortunately, I do not speak Spanish and I am without an interpreter. I wonder if you could interpret for me?"

"I am on my way to Caracas for a vacation," said Manuel, "but because I, too, am a Christian I will be happy to help you." What Manuel did not know was that though the man was an evangelist, he was also a faith healer.

The morning after their first service together, the evangelist asked Manuel if he would like to go to the post office with him. Manuel declined. When the evangelist returned, Manuel saw that he was pale and clearly angry.

"Take this chair and sit down," he ordered. "I want to talk to you. When I was in the post office I met a man who speaks German, Spanish and English."

Manuel smiled. "I also speak three languages," he said quietly.

"That is not my point," said the evangelist angrily. "The man told me he was at our meeting last night and that you did not translate my message correctly. Is that true?"

"Yes," said Manuel firmly. "It is true what the man says."

"Aha! So that's why no one came forward for healing last night."

"Yes," said Manuel. "That is right. When you asked the people how many wanted to come forward for healing, I turned it around and said, 'How many want to accept the Lord Jesus Christ.' When a few raised their hands, I said, 'Fine, but don't come to the altar. Just stay where you are and at the end of the service I will come and speak to you in person.' Now," continued Manuel, lowering his voice, "before we go any further, I am going to tell you why I didn't translate your message exactly the way you gave it."

Manuel straightened in his chair and pointed a bold finger at the evangelist. "The reason," said Manuel, "is because you said that you had the power to heal and I do not agree to that! I do not agree to that!" Manuel's normally quiet, gracious humility gave over to a titanic presence before which the evangelist sat dumb. Manuel's words were never out of control but he uttered them with such force of conviction that the evangelist felt he had been spiked.

"Do you believe what you preach?"

"Yes," said the evangelist weakly, "I do."

"Fine. I will stay with you until the week is over. But," and Manuel fixed the evangelist with a strong, steady gaze, "you must give credit to God."

9

"Please Tie My Shoes"

"How would you like to help paint the new workshop rooms?" asked Richard Anderson, the energetic Wycliffe linguist from Canada.

"Sure," said Manuel good-naturedly. "I am strong now from my vacation in Caracas and I always enjoy my trip to Ixmiquilpan. Besides I have a few weeks before I hear about my scholarship from the United Nations."

Manuel's five-foot-four stature needed the help of a three-legged stool to reach the poured concrete ceilings of the workshop room. With a soggy paint roller, he applied the light green paint across the gray cement surface, reaching out as far as he could with each stroke. On one stroke he over-reached and lost his balance. Richie heard the noise of Manuel's fall and rushed into the room. Manuel was prostrate on his back and wincing in pain.

"Are you all right?" Richie asked anxiously.

"My back, my back," groaned Manuel. "I can't move!"

The doctor in the Mexico City hospital shook his head. "I'm sorry, gentlemen," he said, "but Señor Arenas has a broken back. He will be in a body cast for at least six months."

The delay in his formal education Manuel accepted as the will of God. And he graciously smiled through the pain. But for some reason his stomach didn't. A tiny ulcer was beginning to form in the lining of his stomach.

Finding the road to recovery abrasively slow for his active personality, Manuel spent the inactive hours perfecting his French and German. Herman Aschmann, in from the tribe for a few months, became Manuel's nurse, bathing him, tying his shoes and encouraging him when he became discouraged.

Part of Manuel's later therapy, as ordered by the doctor, was to practice walking, initially several blocks a day and gradually increasing the distance to a maximum of fifteen blocks. On one of these walks about four months after his accident, Manuel, in penguin fashion, walked to Sanborn's House of Tile restaurant to buy a *Time* magazine. As he was crossing the street after making his purchase, he noticed both his shoes were untied.

"Well," he thought, "I will ask a shoeshine boy to tie them for me." But when he reached Alameda Park he saw only one boy, and a number of people were waiting for him. Wearied by his long walk and conscious of the increasing weight of his cast, Manuel didn't feel he could wait until the boy had finished. Then he spied a policeman walking up the street.

"Excuse me, sir," said Manuel politely, "would you be so kind as to help me?"

"Of course," answered the policeman, delighted to be asked for assistance. "What can I do for you? Are you lost?"

"No, I am not lost. I know the city well. It is just—well, would you be so kind as to tie my shoes?"

For an instant Manuel's voice seemed not to have registered. Then as though he had been slapped across the mouth, the policeman showed the indignity of Manuel's words. His eyes opened wide in instant hate and he actually sputtered.

"Sir," said Manuel calmly, "what I want is if you could help me to tie my shoes."

This time the policeman spat an insult at Manuel by using the Spanish familiar form of "you" (tú), "You are crazy!"

Manuel smiled. "Sir, please don't think I am crazy or that I am joking with you. Look at my cast." With that Manuel unbuttoned his shirt.

"Thank you for helping me," said Manuel after the policeman had tied the shoes. "Here is the tip, and I want to also give you this."

Under the shade of tall eucalyptuses, the two walked slowly to the end of the park while the policeman read *Four Things God Wants You to Know.* At the corner the policeman asked Manuel for another tract.

"I am sorry," said Manuel, "that is all I have. Did you like it?"

"Yes," said the policeman, a faraway look in his eyes. "It talks about God."

"Well, would you like to have some coffee with me and hear more?"

"Yes," answered the policeman, "I would."

In the downstairs restaurant of the Hotel Regis, Manuel and the policeman talked. When they parted more than two hours later, the policeman gripped Manuel's hand warmly. "A thousand thanks for asking me to tie your shoes. If you hadn't, I would never have come to know the Lord!"

Six months later, Manuel pushed the entrance buzzer on the big metal gate at Wycliffe headquarters. Just before the gate opened Manuel heard a shout from behind. Hurrying toward him was a policeman.

"Hey," he called, "aren't you the one who led me to the Lord?"

Manuel smiled a big, warm smile. "Yes, yes, I am. So glad to see you again!"

"Oh," said the policeman excitedly, "I'm also very glad to see you. Please be good enough to stay right here five minutes and I will be right back."

"Let's talk now."

"No, no, no!" said the policeman emphatically. "I'm going to talk to you, but within five minutes."

Perplexed, Manuel watched him race around the corner in the direction of the local police station. In about five minutes the policeman returned. But what Manuel saw made his stomach churn with fear. Beside his policeman friend walked five others.

"You remember when we were in the restaurant?" said the policeman. "I forgot to get your address. After I got on a bus I sat wondering if I would ever see you again. Then a man sat down beside me and of all things began to witness to me. I told him I had just this minute accepted the Lord. 'Good,' said the man. 'I am a pastor and if you have accepted the Lord then I want to invite you to come to our church on Sunday.'

"So I went. But all the time I never forgot how you loved me. Now I want to show you that your love is not in vain. Please meet five men who came to accept the Lord because you asked me to tie your shoes."

The book was heavy and thick but Herman, Manuel and Larry Puckett, a boyish-looking missionary with the Mexican Indian Mission, didn't mind carrying quantities of them over the rugged Totonac mountain trails. It was 1959, shortly after Manuel's cast had been removed, and the men were distributing the recently published Totonac New Testament.

Since that gloomy confrontation with his father fifteen years earlier, Manuel's visits to his village had been infrequent and of short duration. He would wait at the Aschmann home until his father left for the cornfield. Then he would make a quick dash to his mother's home and spend a few hours visiting and explaining the way of salvation. It was through these short visits that Luz gradually came to understand the full meaning of Manuel's favorite Scripture verses, John 3:16 and 14:6.

"What shall I do with my idols?" she asked Manuel one day. "I don't trust them any more."

Fearing his mother might tell her neighbors he told her to sell them, Manuel said, "If you really trust the Lord you must ask Him."

After his arrival in Zapotitlán to begin the distribution of the Totonac New Testament, Manuel paid his customary call on his mother.

"Hello, my son. Do you remember when I asked you about my gods? I just want to tell you the true God gave me the answer. Even though I had eighteen idols and paid fifty pesos for each one, I burned all but one."

"Why did you keep one?" questioned Manuel.

"Because," said Luz, "your father told me I must keep just one for him."

To Manuel's extreme delight he discovered his mother's faith in Christ was meaningful and alive. Even though Mariano would not allow her to attend church services, Luz had visited the Aschmann home. Under Bessie's tutelage she learned hymns and choruses and began memorizing numerous Scripture passages.

At first, her neighbors accused her of worshipping the devil. "You must believe in the devil," they would say. "We can't see God anywhere in your house."

"No," said Luz, "that is not true. I now have the true God living in my own heart."

"In her own quiet, sweet way," said Bessie to Manuel later, "your mother has developed a strong effective witness for the Lord."

Coming now as an observer, Manuel discovered that most of the Totonacs in his valley had changed. Of two thousand people, more than one thousand met regularly in the white stone church to worship the true God. Women no longer spent a week's wages in a night on liquor. The crippling fear of offending idols and evil spirits of the forest was also gone from most homes. In the place of fear was a jubilant expression of Christian love and confidence.

The trip into his green hills was also a time of personal discovery for Manuel. For years his energies had been directed toward acquiring as much academic training as possible. His schooling in Mexico, Canada and the United States, together with a deep involvement with people of other cultures, was fast making him a citizen of the world. Names like Istanbul, Jerusalem, Sweden, Hamburg, London, Algiers, Prague, Tokyo, Rome, Venezuela, São Paulo and others were frequent postmarks on Manuel's correspondence. There were also men of influence in companies like Lufthansa and American Airlines who frequently offered Manuel comfortable job opportunities. In each instance the job offers were deliciously tempting. Often uncertain of his ultimate role, Manuel frequently saw no real reason for not seriously considering some of the positions offered.

"I have known hunger and poverty," he would reason. "Why can't I serve the Lord just as effectively with a good paying job as teacher, government worker or businessman."

But for some reasons unknown to himself he always felt unsatisfied with the dream. Yet it had bothered him just a little that after his graduation at Dallas Bible College his friends automatically assumed he would return to the Totonacs. To their surprise Manuel announced he wasn't ready for the Totonacs yet. "I am going instead," he said, "to the University of Chicago to work on my bachelor's degree."

After graduating with an A.B. in Education from the University of Chicago he was still unsure of God's ultimate role for him.

"I have asked my good friend Dr. Carlos Gonzalez, who is now practicing medicine in Madrid, to help me get a scholarship from the United Nations."

This announcement left most of his friends sure he would never return to the Totonacs. A few well-meaning people even approached the Aschmanns and pleaded with them to advise Manuel against going. They argued that he had attended the Summer Institute of Linguistics, a business college and Dallas Bible College, and had a degree from the University of Chicago. He spoke Totonac, Spanish, Aztec, French, German and Italian, and had more training than most of them had. Surely he was ready now to return to his people.

Good-naturedly the Aschmanns would simply smile and say, "We can't tell him what to do. Let's wait, pray and trust the Lord." Unknown to Herman, his homespun advice was to reap great dividends. Observing the conspicuous moral and spiritual improvement brought about by the Scriptures in Totonac, Manuel realized the goal of Bible translation was just now beginning.

While they distributed New Testaments, Herman and Larry talked of the obvious need of quality men to pastor many of the newly formed churches and chapels throughout the Totonac hills. "It is unfortunate," said Herman, "that when there are men who show leadership, there are no schools in Totonac that can give them the kind of training they need."

"What do you mean?" questioned Larry.

"Well," said Herman thoughtfully, "most Totonac churches are unable to support their pastors. When a young man goes to Bible school outside of the tribe, he usually returns feeling the importance of his education. He further expects, as he has been taught, that a congregation should support him. What we need is a school that will give Totonac men practical training that can be used right in the tribe. If a man wants to be a pastor, he should also be taught how to be a basket maker or a barber or a carpenter or learn something about animal husbandry. If he could learn skills that are geared to Totonac needs, along with Bible training, we would have a powerful corps of young men to lead our believers."

"What do you think, Manuel? Do you agree?"

"Yes, yes," said Manuel thoughtfully, "I agree, I agree to that."

Outwardly Manuel was passive, but inside the idea of helping with or teaching in a school for Totonacs fired his imagination. He wondered if this was why the Lord had him come on this trip.

But it was really the second event some months later which showed Manuel unequivocally that the responsibility for specialized training among the Totonacs would have to be his.

Manuel was neatly dressed in gray trousers, brown suede shoes, a checked sport shirt and a pork pie rain hat. He looked as if he were ready for an afternoon of golf. Actually he was setting out on a two-day hike over muddy jungle trails. His partner, an American dentist who had offered to do some dental work among the Totonac villages, puffed along in hiking boots and dungarees.

"That's strange," said Manuel.

"What's strange?" asked the dentist.

"That Totonac man over by the big rock. He's crying!"

"Why do you weeps?" asked Manuel.

The Indian looked hopelessly pathetic as he raised a tear-stained face to Manuel's question. "The Spaniard in the hacienda cheated me when I sold him my pigs," said the Indian.

"How did he cheat you?"

"He gave me five one-hundred peso bills instead of five one-thousand peso bills. And because I can't read or write I couldn't tell the difference. After I came out of the hacienda, I asked a Mexican merchant to count my money and he told me how much I had."

"Come with me," said Manuel. "We will visit the hacienda. When we do, I want you to stay outside the gate."

Always happy for visitors and news of the outside world, the Spaniard gave Manuel and the dentist a warm welcome. After a cool drink, and a tour of the Spaniard's lands and cattle stalls, Manuel announced the reason for their visit.

"I am sorry to say," said Manuel, when the tour was over, "that my visit to your house is not for pleasure."

"Oh?" said the Spaniard.

"No," said Manuel, "I have business to talk with you. There was a man on the trail who said you cheated him in the sale of some pigs. Is that the truth?"

The color drained from the Spaniard's face, his eyes narrowed. "No!" he said angrily. "It is not true. The man is a liar!"

"I don't think so," said Manuel coolly. "I will bring the man in so you can remember if you cheated him or not."

Slowly and timidly the Indian entered the courtyard when Manuel called. "This is the man who said he was cheated," said Manuel.

The Spaniard gave a nervous laugh; then with an offhand swing of his arm said, "He is just an ignorant Indian. Why bother to help him? Let him remain in his ignorance."

"Why not help him?" said Manuel, his eyes leveled straight at the Spaniard. "This man has done nothing wrong. It is you who have done the wrong."

The Spaniard gathered his thoughts together and said in a self-assured voice, "Why do you bother with this matter? It is, after all, none of your business."

"True," said Manuel, "what you say is true. It is not my business. This man is not my brother, in fact I don't know his name or where he lives. And he doesn't know my name." Manuel lowered his voice and continued to speak in a firm voice. "But it hurts me what you have done to him. Now, once more I want to ask you, is it true that you cheated this poor Indian?"

Again the Spaniard became angry. "No!" he yelled, "he is a liar! It is none of your business!"

"I am afraid that is not so," said Manuel. "The Indian told me the truth. You are the liar. This now is my business."

"Look," said the Spaniard. "I will give you two hundred pesos just to shut up and go away."

"I am not interested in your money," said Manuel. "I am interested in justice."

"If you don't take the money," asked the Spaniard, "what will you do?"

Manuel fixed his eyes on the Spaniard. "I will go directly to the supreme court! I will go to the supreme court. It doesn't matter if I spend my own money. It is not right what you have done to this poor Indian man who cannot read or write."

Scarcely able to understand what was happening, the Indian stood in dumb silence as the Spaniard counted out four thousand and five hundred pesos and plunked them into his hand.

"Thank you," said Manuel politely. "You are so kind."

"It's too bad," said the dentist when they were once more on the trail, "there isn't some way for these Totonacs to have a school in their own language so they wouldn't have to be cheated."

"They will," said Manuel. "They will have one someday."

10

Helga

The tugs, toy-like on the water far below, pushed and pulled the German liner *Berlin* into sailing position in the main channel of the Hudson River. As if to give the ship one final boost on its nine-day voyage to Bremerhaven, the tug gave three short farewell blasts on their shrill steam whistles.

It was early in September, 1961. Fascinated with his new experience, Manuel watched the tugs plow back through the dull waters to begin their work all over again. "Thank You, Lord," he said, "for giving me the scholarship and letting me go to the University of Erlangen." Manuel opened his eyes, breathed a generous gulp of fresh sea air, and turned to find his cabin.

"Excuse me," said a young man in German. "Would you help me find my cabin?"

"Yes," said Manuel, "I will. I am also trying to find mine."

"You speak very nice German," said the man with a smile. "Where did you learn it?"

"In Mexico City and at the University of Chicago," answered Manuel.

"How wonderful," the German said with rising interest, "to meet someone who speaks my language. How about meeting me tonight at 8:00 in the cocktail lounge so we can become better acquainted."

"Very good," said Manuel. "Thank you."

There were eight young men singing lusty songs and gulping steins of beer. Manuel smiled. He had never seen people sing and rejoice like this before. "Ah," said his German friend when he noticed Manuel, "a beer for our Mexican friend. Come and join us."

Smiling politely, Manuel thanked his friend for the beer but asked if it would be all right if he just drank a Coke or a ginger ale. His new friend wouldn't hear of it, insisting that Manuel drink beer with the rest.

"I am sorry," said Manuel with a firmness that momentarily jolted his friend. "I would like just to have a ginger ale." The young German smiled weakly and wondered what kind of person would rather drink ginger ale than beer.

If his German friend had doubts about Manuel before the voyage, there were none at the end. For nine days Manuel shared his faith with more than 500 passengers. So impressed were they with his character and honest concern for them as individuals that 375 later sent him a personal invitation for Christmas dinner. Manuel said later, "Because I didn't want to hurt anyone, I sent them each a card and told them I was going to Turkey."

During the Middle Ages, Nuremberg was Germany's most important cultural center. Today it still retains vivid memories of its golden age of higher learning and culture. The gothic buildings of the University of Erlangen, the huge medieval wine cellars turned into a college dormitory, the Kaiserburg—all reminded Manuel of Tajin, the ancient Totonac pyramids in faraway Mexico.

Instantly Manuel felt a deep cultural affinity and fell hopelessly in love with Germany, its language and its people. One of the people he fell in love with had long flaxen hair, light blue eyes and freckles across her angular nose. Her name was Helga and he met her at the university. In that mysterious way known only to young people, they were attracted to each other. It was an old world romance. Band concerts in the park, excursions up the Pegnitz River to a restaurant for dinner, and lingering talks over coffee and *Lebkuchen* in a quiet coffee-house where three hours passed like three minutes.

It was a painful kind of love that left Manuel weak and sick inside when he was away from Helga. When they were together, the pain stopped. Her presence was like a soothing balm, and Manuel felt warm and comfortable. There was talk of marriage after graduation, but each time Manuel told Helga of his dream for the Totonacs, he noticed a strange smile creep across her face. It wasn't until they had been going together for sometime that he realized that she had no intention of ever living among the Totonacs. The thought of losing her stabbed him like a hot knife, but he knew what he must do.

"It's better that you live in Germany," he said tenderly as they walked along the riverbank. "It is hot in Mexico. There are bugs and I don't think you would be happy there. I know God wants me to return to my people. I must keep my promise to God and share my faith and education with them. And always it is better for both of us to find God's best for our lives rather than just the good."

Almost as quickly as it started, the romance was over, at least academically.

"An ulcer!" exclaimed Manuel. "How would I get an ulcer?"

"From overwork," answered the doctor, "or too much worry, or too many emotional problems or upsets."

"Oh," said Manuel to himself, "I wonder if Helga—" Interrupting Manuel's thoughts with instructions to substitute tea for coffee and to remove spicy food from his diet, the doctor concluded with a suggestion that Manuel take a vacation.

"Thank you," said Manuel graciously, "I leave for Turkey in the morning."

Manuel relaxed in his seat in the plane and reread a portion of a letter he had received a few months earlier.

> I am so very anxious to meet the one through whom this unworthy Turkish family has come to know such complete happiness. Would you honor our house by spending your Christmas vacation with Kurtartt, myself and family? I am enclosing a round-trip plane ticket.

It was signed by Kurtartt's father.

The reunion with Kurtartt was filled with the telling and retelling of how Manuel befriended and finally won Kurtartt to the Lord. Finally, when the conversation gave way to munching on the *boreks* and sipping the thick, sweet

Turkish coffee, Manuel said, "Since you are Turkish, I want to tell you a Turkish story!"

It was the morning after members of the Wycliffe Bible Translators and myself were on a television program in Mexico City. The Department of Education had asked Wycliffe to explain about its work among the Indian tribes, and I had spoken about the newly translated Totonac New Testament. I was eating breakfast the following morning when a man called me on the telephone.

"I saw you on television last night, and I would like to meet you. Can you come to my house for lunch?" I said I could, and he gave me an address in a nice section of the city, about an hour from where I was staying.

"The reason I called and invited you to my house," he said when I arrived, "was because of what you said on television last night." Surprised and a little afraid, I asked him what I had said. "You said that your language is almost like Turkish." I replied it was true and asked why he questioned the statement.

"Because," he answered, "I am Turkish and I wonder if you can speak my language." When I told him I didn't, he asked angrily, "Then why do you compare Turkish with Totonac?" And I told him of my friendship with Kurtartt.

"Oh," he exclaimed, "I am also a doctor!"

When I told him I had read the Koran, he was more surprised. We had a long discussion on the differences between the Koran and the Bible and the differences between Jesus Christ and Mohammed. He was so interested in what I said that he asked me to come back. After three or four visits I asked him to come with me to a doctor's convention that was being held at a lake near Mexico City. He came, and that weekend another doctor friend of mine and I led him to the Lord.

Kurtartt's father smiled, shook his gray head slowly and wondered aloud how it was that a little Indian could be such a remarkable instrument for God.

After Turkey, it was Switzerland, Spain, Sweden, Hungary, Germany, France and Italy. But of all, it was his visits to East Germany that were among Manuel's most memorable.

On his first visit he was confronted by a long line of cars and pedestrians waiting to pass through the narrow check point separating East and West Germany. Manuel, who was no stranger to border crossings and official red tape, declined to take a place at the end of the line. "Come," he said to Charles Wickersham, a young U.S. army private from Georgia, "there is no sense to waiting in a long line," and went directly to the officer in charge.

"So you are Mexican," said the officer.

"Yes," responded Manuel with a bright smile, "I am."

"Well, then you do not have to wait in line. You and your friend may pass through immediately." Reacting like a true Latin, Manuel reached into his wallet and pulled out two marks. The officer raised both hands in protest, declaring he was not permitted to take gratuities.

"But," said Manuel, "I want to give you something to show my appreciation."

"Well," said the officer, clearing his throat and eyeing Manuel's tooled leather wallet, "your purse is very nice."

"Oh," said Manuel, "This wallet is too old."

"It doesn't matter. I will take it."

"No," said Manuel with a firm smile, "not this one. But the next time I come I will bring you a new one."

True to his word, on his second trip, Manuel gave the officer a new hand-tooled Mexican wallet. Immediately they were friends. On subsequent crossings, the officer would smile and say how happy he was to see his Mexican friend. After a perfunctory search of Manuel's suitcase, he would give Manuel a good-natured slap on the back and wave him through. Never once did he ask about the half-dozen German Bibles Manuel carried.

Accustomed to vibrant, enterprising Mexicans and West Germans, Manuel's view of East Germany was gloomy. Subconsciously, he expected the same flamboyant advertising on stores and buildings that he saw in the West. Instead he saw cold numbers in place of proprietors' names.

But the real gloom came when Manuel visited an underground church. "There were about twenty young people," he said later, "about eighteen to twenty-five years of age. No one sang. They were afraid the neighbors would hear and tell the authorities. We sat in a circle. Each one read a passage of Scripture from a badly worn Bible that was passed from hand to hand. After that we prayed, and then the service was over. They were happy to meet me, and when I gave out the new Bibles there were tears. I told them of Mexico and explained that Indian believers also suffer for their faith. As I left to go they asked me to visit them again because they frequently felt as though God had forgotten them but that my visit helped them to understand He hadn't!"

Manuel's friends in Europe never once doubted his intention to realize the dream of a Bible technical school for the Totonacs. Whenever he had the opportunity, he explained his plan to all who would listen. But sometimes, when an especially appealing position was offered, Manuel's vision became momentarily clouded. This was never more true than with the position offered to him by a mathematics professor from Barcelona.

Each summer hundreds of Spaniards flocked north over the Pyrenees in search of better paying jobs in Germany. The spiritual welfare of the many migrant Spanish workers in Nuremberg was cared for by a Spanish-speaking church located in the Spanish colony. It was at this church that Manuel served a part of his free time as interim pastor, and it was here that he met Professor Carrillo. When the professor learned of Manuel's program in education and past academic training, he pleaded with Manuel to return with him to Spain.

"Spain is in desperate need of qualified teachers," he would say. "I can assure you of an immediate position in any one of our high schools or colleges in Barcelona or Madrid." Then, with a painful, agonizing grimace and a voice full of emotion, the professor concluded his argument with, "Manuel, you are strong. You have many years of service for the Lord, but my body is weak. I am dying of cancer. Could you not come for just one year?"

Manuel told the story at his farewell sermon after receiving his degree at Erlangen. After referring to the offer as the most tempting he had ever received, he said, "When Professor Carillo explained how deeply I was needed and how I could substitute for him right away, I wanted the job. I told myself that here was something for me right now. The Totonac school was a faraway dream that would take years to accomplish, and besides, where would I get the money I would need to build it. I thought maybe I could earn some teaching school.

"But then I remembered a man crying on a jungle trail after someone had cheated him on the sale of his pigs, because he couldn't read, write or count money. I remembered my own mother and how a selfish landlord cheated her out of her land and gave her only a tiny fraction of its true value. I remembered also my promise to the Lord as a young boy: that if He gave me an education, I would take it back and share it with my people. Now in a few days I leave this wonderful country with your prayers and a dream. I also leave with a greater desire to help the Totonacs learn to read and write and understand the full love of the Lord Jesus Christ."

After the service, as Manuel stood in front of the church and shook the hands of his friends and well-wishers, he was approached by a little girl of nine.

"My grandmother gave this."

"What did she give you?" asked Manuel with a smile.

"She gave me four marks for a new doll. But since my old doll is still good, I am going to give you this for your Bible school."

The next day, when the dignified German bank teller asked him how much he wished to deposit in his new savings account, Manuel opened his wallet and counted out the four German marks (the equivalent of one U.S. dollar) and pushed them under the glass window.

II

Pavilion of 2,000 Tribes

On a Sunday afternoon the New York subway is a ghost of its weekday self. Half-empty cars rattle and squeak as they speed along burnished tracks. People who are unaccustomed to a mixture of heat, ozone, leftover air and intermittent lurching, often find a strong catalyst occurring in their stomach. Each time the train stopped and started, Manuel bumped one or the other of two Negro couples who sat next to him. He was hot, and he wondered why they sat so close when other seats were available.

"I wonder," asked Manuel of one of the couples, "if you could help me."

"Sure, man," one of the men replied, "what do you need?"

"I'm not feeling too well," said Manuel gently, "and I am wondering if I am near my stop. I am looking for Stone Street."

"Well, man, you is lucky. Stone is near where we get off and that happens to be the next stop. We will just take you there."

"Thank you," said Manuel politely. "That would be so kind."

The long, dimly lit ramp would have caused most New Yorkers to become uneasy and suspicious. Not Manuel. He had no reason to doubt the integrity of his guides—not until they all turned a corner. The two couples mounted a swift, well-executed attack. Something smashed into Manuel's mouth. Instantly his mind flashed back to the Zócalo in Mexico City, but only for an instant before it snapped off. Someone landed a quick judo chop to his neck and he dropped.

It was forty-five minutes before Manuel regained consciousness. This time there were no dazzling lights, soft music or women in white. Just a dank tunnel of a ramp. There was one similarity. His teeth were missing. Fortunately, this time it was his bridge. He knew where he was, but his wallet was gone. As he limped up the ramp, he wondered if God really wanted him to take part in Wycliffe's pavilion.

(Manuel had been asked by Cameron Townsend to take part in the New York World's Fair before he left Germany. Explaining that the Wycliffe Translators were to have a building called the Pavilion of 2,000 Tribes, Mr. Townsend said he knew of no other person who could explain the results of Bible translation better than Manuel.)

In spite of the unhappy subway incident, the two years in New York were among Manuel's most fruitful. Albert Williams, Wycliffe's good-natured tour captain at the pavilion, said later that Manuel played an indispensable role in explaining Wycliffe's work. "He conducted all the German and Spanish tours. When the tours were over, many people came back to tell us how amazed they were that this little Indian could speak German so well." Al also recalled the day the Italian came to the pavilion. They were trying to explain to him that no one spoke his language, when Manuel offered to give it a try and took the man on a complete tour of the building.

"Manuel was so good," continued Al, "we worked him during the busiest part of the day. I sometimes felt guilty about this because I knew he suffered pain from his old back injury when he became tired. But even on weekends when we worked him two six-hour shifts, he never complained. He always smiled and showed himself eager to talk. We appreciated this because when we had difficult customers it was Manuel who did the talking."

There was for example the anthropologist who demanded to know why they didn't leave the Indians alone. "Why teach them about Christianity? It isn't good to explain things that are different from their own religion." It was Manuel who answered. Speaking slowly and showing great respect for the man's words, he asked the anthropologist how it was that he knew so much about the Indians. Had he ever lived with them?

"No," said the man, "but I have read what happens when other religions come into a foreign culture."

"I am sorry," said Manuel, "but I haven't read these books so I don't know what they say. But I have lived with Indians and I am one of them. So I can't agree with you that they are happy with the way they live. Now let me ask you another question. Are you satisfied with the way you live?"

"No," said the man thoughtfully. "I suppose not."

"Well," said Manuel tenderly, "if you are not satisfied

with your life here in America, why do you believe Indians in South America and Mexico, who live in ignorance and fear, should be happy. They are just like you. They are humans with the same needs you have."

The anthropologist thanked Manuel, took his name and address and walked out. No one guessed there would be a sequel, until a few days later when Al asked Manuel whom he knew in Cleveland and handed him a letter.

Commenting that he had no friends there, Manuel opened the letter.

> Dear Manuel,
>
> I don't know if you will remember me, but a few months ago I gave you a bad time at the Wycliffe Pavilion. I was the one who said you shouldn't teach Indians about Christianity. Then, you remember, you asked me if I was happy in my life. [Manuel chuckled out loud, "Oh, yes! Yes, I remember this man well."] I related this incident to a fellow teacher one day in the staff lunchroom. When I finished my story, my friend just smiled. Then he asked me the same question! To make a long story short, Manuel, my associate turned out to be a Christian and subsequently led me to the Lord. I just want to thank you for your beautiful patience with me that day and also to tell you I now know what it means to have a satisfied life. Keep up the good work!
>
> ALAN GUILMORE

Another of Manuel's "conquests" was the man who loudly and angrily proclaimed his hatred of missionaries and accused the exhibit and those associated with it of stupidity. Manuel simply smiled. It was a warm innocent kind of smile. The kind that makes one want to smile back.

"What happened to make you so upset?" asked Manuel quietly.

"Well," sputtered the distinguished looking gentleman, "it's those girls! Those girls made me mad."

"Why?" asked Manuel gently.

"I am opposed to anyone who changes the culture of poor Indians and that's what they do when they translate the Bible. Why don't they leave the Indians alone? Look what happened to the Indians in the United States! Look how the Americans stole their land and put them on reservations and that's just what you people are trying to do! I hate it!"

Manuel, in a soft voice full of honest concern for the man said, "Why do you talk like that? Have you seen an American recently who took away land from an Indian?"

"No, no!" said the man, "but I have been to India and Africa and I have seen what the English and Americans have done."

"I am so ignorant," said Manuel. "Tell me what they have done."

"Well," the man said in a voice not quite so angry, "for one thing they have introduced the Protestant religion to these people."

"Yes, you are right," said Manuel. "The people you saw here in this pavilion are the ones who carry God's Word to different cultures. But the difference is, they never force anyone to believe. They do not do what the Spaniards did to the Indians when they first came to Mexico or South

America. When Indians accept Christianity it is because they want to." Manuel then went on to explain something of his own life, after which the man thanked him.

"I understand now," the man said. "I wish the others had talked to me like this. Your speech is very nice. Now I must go."

"Listen, sir," said Manuel, "if I were you, I would not go until you have seen the murals. They illustrate the life of a South American Indian tribe both before and after its conversion. I am sure the murals and accompanying narration will give you an even better understanding."

"Thank you," said the man, "but I don't have much time. I really must go."

"Listen!" Manuel continued, undeterred, "If you don't have time to see the murals, you should at least buy this book." He held up a copy of *Tariri, My Story*. "It tells you all about the murals and Wycliffe work in South America. We sell it for five dollars but I will sell it to you for three."

The man laughed, "You're a great fellow." He bought the book, and turned to leave.

"Now that you have bought the book," said Manuel childlike in his persistence, "you should really see the murals. The next performance is just about to start. I will open the gate and you will be the first inside."

"Look!" the man said. "I bought the book. I really must go."

"Listen," Manuel sounded as if he were about to give away a secret. "If you go in, you don't have to stay for the whole performance. If you don't like it, come back and tell me."

Unable to free himself from Manuel's innocent charms, the man sighed and surrendered with, "All right, all right, you win. But I am coming out in five minutes if I don't like it." Manuel smiled to himself. He knew he had won.

"You were right," said the man after the mural presentation. "I enjoyed it very much. Now I have something for your work." Without another word, he jammed a piece of paper into Manuel's hands, turned and walked out. Manuel unfolded the check and walked over to the cash desk.

"Here," he said to the cashier. "A man gave me one hundred dollars for the work of Bible translation."

After New York, Manuel made a quick trip to Dallas where he was honored by Dallas Bible College as Alumnus of the Year. The following day he left for Chicago to take part in a Wycliffe deputation program. Halfway to the airport, he discovered he had left his only suit hanging in his host's closet.

The cab driver rushed him back to the house and out to the airport in record time. With five minutes to spare, Manuel boarded the plane. He chided himself for being forgetful. The plane appeared full and he was unable to find the empty seat he knew was there. On his second walk through passengers still standing in the aisle, he noticed toward the rear an aisle seat that was empty but for a pile of books. The window seat was occupied by a man.

"Excuse me, sir," Manuel said politely, "is this seat taken? May I remove these books?"

The man looked up at Manuel. His eyes smiled, but there was no spoken reply. Observing that the man's clothes appeared European, Manuel tried French. The eyes smiled again, but there was no vocal response. Manuel tried German, and this time the man responded. The books were removed and Manuel fastened his belt just before the jet pulled itself into the sky and headed for Chicago. Aloft, Manuel continued to talk to the man in German. After a few minutes he noticed the man spoke with an accent.

"What work do you do and where are you from?" asked Manuel.

"I am a teacher at the University of Madrid." At which Manuel laughed happily and clapped his hands together. "Why are we speaking in German?" he said excitedly. "I am from Mexico and I speak Spanish!" Whereupon both men switched to Spanish and enjoyed a long conversation.

Fifteen minutes before the plane landed at O'Hare, Manuel said to his companion, "Since you are from Spain, you must be Catholic."

"Yes, I am."

"Good," said Manuel. "Please tell me about your relationship to the Lord Jesus Christ."

The conversation was pleasant. Each shared his faith briefly without hostility or rancor. When the jet came to rest at its disembarking stall, the Spaniard reached out and touched Manuel's arm.

"I wonder," he said thoughtfully, "if you would care to take another fifteen minutes and explain to me more fully the concept of personally accepting Jesus Christ."

"I would be most happy to," said Manuel. "Let's go to a coffee shop."

The airport lunch counter was crowded and noisy. But to Manuel and the Spaniard it seemed as if they were completely alone. After Manuel had explained how one could find Christ personally, both men knelt by their chairs. In that moment, oblivious to the clatter of dishes and coffee cups, the Spaniard voluntarily yielded his will to Christ.

Manuel gave his new friend the names and addresses of Christian friends in Madrid, and then with a long, meaningful *abrazo,* the two parted.

Two weeks later Manuel received a short direct letter from the Spaniard in Madrid.

Dear Manuel,

Please find enclosed one hundred dollars for your work.

JOSE PATINO

P.S. You will be happy to know I have won my father to the Lord.

"I was mad at myself for forgetting my suit," said Manuel in a sermon given a year later to a small church in Mexico City. "But I know now it was all in God's plan. Especially since I received another letter yesterday from my friend and he told me he has now won forty-five people to the Lord."

12

Operation Totonac

It was Manuel's third visit to the small ranch house with the red tile roof. Its owner, a strong, resolute Mexican woman, was also the owner of fourteen acres of land Manuel wanted for his Bible school.

"I think you try to soften me with this gift of mangoes so I will sell my land," said the woman with a laugh.

"Well," said Manuel slightly embarrassed, "it is true. Of all the many places I have searched for land, yours is best for the Totonac school."

"It is the only flat piece of land in the whole valley," said the woman emphatically. "I cannot possibly sell it."

Manuel made two more visits several weeks apart. Each time he brought a gift, one time a box of apples, another time a box of Sanborn's chocolates. On his sixth visit, Manuel brought a cake.

"This is for your birthday," he said with a smile.

"For my birthday!" said the woman in a surprised voice. "How did you know it was my birthday?"

"I asked your son," said Manuel.

"My son is not here to celebrate my birthday," she said,

a tear in her eye, "but you, a stranger, have honored me. Please come in, and eat with me."

"Are you still looking for land?" asked the woman after they finished their meal.

"Yes, I am."

"Do you really need the land?"

"Yes, I do."

"Then," and the woman smiled, "I will sell it to you."

From Texas and Tananarive, from Spain and San Francisco, Grand Forks and Germany, Indianapolis and Italy, Ankara and Alaska and from countries and places in between the money came. A man living in a small community outside San Francisco started Operation Totonac with a few of his friends. They pledged $2.00 per week for the school. After visiting the school property in June, 1967, a group of teen-agers from Devington First Baptist Church in Indianapolis raised $900 for construction costs.

As part of a fund-raising drive, students from John Brown University entered floats in the Siloam Springs annual Christmas parade and raised over $4,000. Impressed with the notion of becoming personally involved, thirty of the students spent their Christmas vacation to help build part of the Bible school. Students of a former Bible study group in Nuremberg had added regularly to Manuel's four marks, which grew to $900 before it was needed.

To thank the many donors and to inform them of the uses of their gifts, Manuel devised a kind of personal newsletter. In one corner, there was a picture of himself standing on a knoll and pointing out over his small valley. The first one was dated August, 1967.

Dear Friends,

Thank you very much for your prayers and help concerning the project of the Totonac Bible School. A year ago it was only a dream. The land was purchased sometime last August. We started to clear the land at the beginning of this year, as well as to buy the materials, such as cement blocks, steel-reinforced cement, wooden beams, etc. The first building of five rooms was begun in April. Praise the Lord that a few days ago it was finished. Now we need to paint it and furnish it.

Some of the friends here have asked me, when is the school going to start, next week or in September? My answer is, I do not know yet. There is still a lot of work to be done. But if it is the Lord's will we would like to start school in January, 1968.

Besides all this, several weeks ago we planted 200 orange trees. Not one of them died. They will start to bear fruit in three years. In a few days we will plant coffee trees. These trees will start to bear in two years. The oranges and coffee that we cannot use we will sell, and use the money for the school.

I will appreciate your prayers that the Lord will make it possible, though we still have to build another building for a kitchen, dining room, etc.

Once again, thank you very much for your prayers. May the Lord bless you all.

Sincerely in Him,

MANUEL ARENAS

A simple declarative progress report to his friends—the Bible school was a reality. But what the letter didn't tell was the pain, frustration, and triumph of the past twelve months.

"You'll need your own transformer, power line and poles," said the Mexican engineer.

"How much will it cost?" asked Manuel.

"About 80,000 pesos," answered the engineer.

"Oh," said Manuel weakly, "I spent most of my money on construction."

"Why don't you see the governor?" said the engineer. "He might give you a discount."

"I will," said Manuel thoughtfully. "I will."

He started his journey at six in the morning. With slow, painful lurches, the bus picked its way around deep potholes, rocks too large to run over and shallow creek beds much as a barefoot man walking on barnacles. After an hour of wheezing and grinding up and down the steep mountain roads, the bus stopped in the town of Villa Juarez.

"Better get some coffee," said the driver. "The bus for Mexico City doesn't leave until ten."

After a three-hour tea break, Manuel boarded the bus for Mexico City. He read for a short distance, but the sharp mountain curves did things to his stomach. At 1:30 in the afternoon he arrived in Mexico City and at 5:00 boarded yet another bus, this one for Puebla City. In Puebla he found a small hotel and then went out for dinner. It was 7:30 P.M.

At 10:00 the following morning, Manuel began his vigil in the governor's large waiting room. Two hours later the governor's secretary told Manuel he couldn't see the governor unless he had a letter of recommendation or someone to formally introduce him.

"Can you introduce me?" asked Manuel innocently.

"No," said the secretary, "but maybe someone in the engineer's office will."

"Manuel! Manuel!" exclaimed two good-looking Mexicans. "What are you doing here?"

To Manuel's surprise the voices came from two former schoolmates. Briefly, Manuel explained his problem.

"Sure," they said. "We will be delighted to arrange an interview."

When Manuel finally obtained an audience and had explained his problem, the governor offered him a 35 percent discount on a power line and transformer. Manuel thanked him and left the ornate chambers. As generous as the discount was it still left the cost far above a thousand dollars, which was all the money he had.

Discouraged but undefeated, Manuel stopped off at Wycliffe headquarters on the way back to the Bible school. "I need two kinds of power," he told his friends. "Electric power for the Bible school and spiritual power for me so I can ask the governor to give me a greater discount."

A week later Manuel made a second trip to Puebla. "No," said the lawyer through whom Manuel was now dealing. "You can't see the governor today. Come back in a week."

A week later the governor was "just too busy." It was suggested he return in a week. In all, he made five tedious trips before his second audience with the governor.

"I thank you for the discount," said Manuel, "but the price is still much too high. I wonder. . . ."

"I am sorry," said the governor, cutting off Manuel's words sharply, "this is no longer in my hands. You must talk to the engineer."

"The governor authorized only a 35 percent discount,"

said the engineer when Manuel asked for a lower price. "If you want a change, you must see him again. Come back in a week and I will see what I can do."

Three months later, Manuel sat in the governor's waiting room conversing with the governor's secretary. "How many trips have you made to Puebla to see the governor since your first interview?" asked the secretary. "Thirty," answered Manuel politely.

In this his third audience with the governor, Manuel changed his tactic. "Sir, the work I am doing is really your work. What I am doing is helping you."

"Oh," said the governor in a surprised voice. "How is what you are doing helping me?"

"Well, you want our country to progress. Isn't that true?"

"Why, uh . . . uh yes, of course!" answered the governor.

"Good," said Manuel. "We both know Mexico can't progress unless the people know how to read and write. Isn't that true?"

"Yes, that's true."

"Isn't it also true," said Manuel, "that the responsibility to teach literacy in your state includes Indians as well?"

"Yes," said the governor weakly, "it is."

"Well," said Manuel with a bright smile, "you should help me do your work. I am opening a school to teach Totonacs to read and write. But how can I begin if I have no electric power? If you would give me the electricity, we can both help Mexico to grow. These Totonacs do not understand Spanish. I can teach them because I first of all understand Totonac. But without a school and people who understand them, these poor Indians will never learn and

Mexico will not progress as fast. With your help, Señor Governor, both of us can help Mexico to grow strong together."

Without a word to Manuel, the governor pressed a button on his desk and called in the engineer with whom Manuel had had previous contact. "Any time you are ready," said the governor softly, "you can install the power line and transformer for Señor Arenas and his Totonac school, free of charge."

One day while on a trip to buy material for the Bible school, Manuel decided to visit a new believer in a village near Papantla. The weather was hot and Manuel was resting briefly under the shade of a banana tree.

"Good morning, and where are you going?" said a cheery voice.

Manuel turned and saw an older man. His face was deeply pockmarked, but his voice was warm and reassuring.

"I am going to the village of Sweetwater," said Manuel in Totonac.

"You speak Totonac really good," said the Indian. "Where did you learn it?"

"Totonac is my language," said Manuel with a smile.

"I don't believe you," said the man. "If you are Totonac, where are your Indian pants?"

"I changed them," said Manuel with a light laugh.

The old man looked at Manuel for a long moment, then said seriously, "I wonder, brother, if you know God. Are you reborn? If you are not, you should be." Then to Manuel's surprise, the Indian began to quote John 3:16.

"How did you learn this verse," asked Manuel, "and how did you become a Christian?"

"Six years ago," said the Indian, "a man in a barber shop in Papantla asked me to buy a New Testament. In those days I couldn't read but I thought perhaps some day I would learn and when I did I thought it would be good to find out what God has to say.

"It took me three years before I learned to read. All that time I kept my New Testament wrapped in my *morral.* One day, after I could read, I found John 3:16. I was impressed with the words, 'should not perish, but have everlasting life.'

"For several months I kept reading the New Testament. Then one night after I read the words of this verse again, I could not sleep. For many hours I lay awake on my straw mat. Finally, I said to myself, 'Do I have everlasting life?' I had to say that I did not. Then after many more hours of thinking, I got out of my bed, knelt down and asked the Lord Jesus to forgive my sins and give me everlasting life. Since that night I have been so thankful because I now know who it is that gives me all the necessary things of life."

The old man paused and brushed the dirt from his white pants.

"Friend," he continued, "I have had such wonderful happiness from my New Testament that I would like to greet the man who made this and thank him personally. I have heard that this man lives in Mexico City and that he comes down here once in a while. If you should ever meet him, please tell him how wonderful this book is and how happy it has made an old Totonac man—you are crying. Why do you cry?"

"I cry," said Manuel, "because I am happy with you and because I once knew what it was to be in darkness."

"We will meet again," said the old man. "The Lord be with you."

Manuel watched him walk down the trail until the jungle greenery swallowed him up. He realized that old man had been referring to Herman Aschmann and that the man's copy of the New Testament was one of the many Herman had sold in those places where Totonacs coming in from their hills might congregate. He wondered if he should have told the old man that he also had worked on the translation and that the reason he cried was because he was so thankful he had not quit working on the New Testament as he had wanted to so many times when he was young.

"Thank You, dear Lord," said Manuel, "for letting me meet this old man. And thank You for letting me come back to my people."

Epilogue

It was June, the month of rain and that time of year when according to Totonac folklore St. Michael is angry and draws his sword.

Sitting on the porch of Manuel's guest house at the Bible school, it was easy to understand why Totonacs believed this! Before the ominous sounds of thunder rolled and cracked across the heavens, I saw erratic streaks of lightning dance across the valley floor. Then like fog rolling in from the sea, great fingers of dark gray clouds swept down between two thimble-shaped mountains and covered the clean, white buildings. When the rain came, it was oppressive and thick. The dank humidity made it hard to breathe and I felt I was being enveloped. From a nearby hut I heard the terrified scream of a child; then a mother chanting.

When finally the rain stopped, I walked along the Spanish colonial-type porch of the dormitory building to visit the newly arrived students. There were eight who had come to study. One was a small oval-faced boy of about eighteen. Manuel was talking quietly to one of the new arrivals. It seemed to me he was taking special pains to reassure the boy of something.

"He walked twelve long hours to come to the school," said Manuel later. Then with a faraway look in his black eyes, he said, "Yes, he walked twelve hours over the mountains. His father told him if he came to the school he was never to come back to his house. When the boy left, his father said, 'I want you to think about what you are doing because if you go to this school, I will completely disinherit you. You will receive not one piece of my land!' "

"What happened when he left?" I asked.

"His father yelled at him and pronounced him disinherited from the family."

"What was the young man's reaction?"

"He just told me," answered Manuel, "he knew he had to serve the Lord no matter what his father did and also because of his promise."

"Promise?"

"Yes," said Manuel. "He promised the Lord he would go back to his people and share his knowledge if the Lord gave him an education."